Closing the Racial Academic Achievement Gap

by Matthew Lynch

Chicago, Illinois

First Edition, First Printing

Front cover illustration by Harold Carr

Copyright © 2006 by Matthew Lynch

All rights reserved.

Printed in the United States of America

ISBN #: 0-974900-06-0

DEDICATION

This book is dedicated to my mother and father, Patsy and Jessie Lynch. You made me realize that growing up poor can be a blessing.

To Mrs. Eubanks: thank you for loving each of your students.

CONTENTS

ACKNOWLEDGEMENTS

I would first like to thank my Creator for allowing me to breathe his air for as long as I have. I would like to thank my parents, Jessie and Patsy Lynch, and my sisters, Angelina and Tammy, for supporting me no matter what. Thanks to my cousin Malcolm for giving me a dose of reality from time to time and to his mother for starting off the tradition of school teachers in our family. Thank you, all of my friends and family, for your support.

I give my thanks to Dr. Bettye McDaniel for hiring me to teach at Hazlehurst Middle School and to all of my colleagues who aided me in my growth as a teacher and a professional. I give my thanks to Dr. Rodney Washington for his inspiration, motivation, and insight, and to Dr. Carrine Bishop, a scholar and revolutionary, for her example.

To the children of world without an advocate, I will fight for you.

PREFACE

The purpose of this book is to present theories, research, and suggested practices that can be used to instruct and discipline African American children. The intended audience is educators, administrators, parents, and all those who are charged with the duty of cultivating the minds of African American children.

The central message of this book is that in spite of the myriad social, ethical, political, and academic problems that tend to tarnish the educational environment, African American children can succeed academically. This book shares the latest theories, research, and practices from the field of education and psychology.

The enactment of the No Child Left Behind Act has ushered in a new era of educational reform. No longer will teachers and administrators be allowed to let children of color fall through the cracks. Teachers, parents, and administrators must become aware of the latest research in multicultural education in order to help African American children realize their full potential, an arduous task for children of any race. This book will seek to assist them in the realization of this goal.

INTRODUCTION

When I was an undergraduate at the University of Southern Mississippi, I had the pleasure of taking a class under Dr. Koeppel entitled "The History of Psychology." He was a capable professor and encouraged his students to maximize their potential. For one of our class research papers, a classmate and I decided to study the subject of race and intelligence. We uncovered startling studies funded by racists and White supremacists concluding that race determined a person's level of intelligence. According to these findings, Caucasians were genetically predisposed to be intellectually superior while African Americans were intellectually inferior. Some of the studies and articles we found were shocking and offensive. One study that particularly alarmed me concluded that the darker a person's skin, the less intelligent he or she was.

During our presentation, I pointed out that according to these studies, since I was the darkest person in the room, I was intellectually inferior to everyone else. However, I had one of the highest averages in my class. I also highlighted a number of studies conducted by African American psychologists that offered empirically-based rebuttals, and their studies concluded that race does not determine a person's cognitive abilities or level of functioning and that the previous studies had no scientific merit. We received an A on the assignment, but I still felt as though we had not done enough.

I consequently devoured all the information I could on the subject of race, genetics, and intelligence. This research was a major impetus for my decision to become a teacher and also a basis for this book. I promptly told my friends that when I graduated, I wanted to return to my hometown to teach in order to make sure that African American children in Hazlehurst would not fall prey to stereotypes, self-fulfilling prophecies, and institutional racism.

When I graduated, I took a teaching position in my hometown of Hazlehurst, Mississippi. Hazlehurst had a dual system of de facto segregation that still thrives: public school for Blacks, private school for Whites. (In order for you to understand the severity of segregation in my hometown, it is imperative that I disclose that 96 percent of Hazlehurst City School's student population was Black, three percent was Hispanic, and one percent or less was Caucasian/other.)

I remember my first day as a teacher just like it was yesterday. I was given a fifth grade class by the principal, Dr. Bettye McDaniel. During a school-wide assembly, I was told to call out the names of my homeroom students over a megaphone. I then escorted them to my room and proceeded to give them a speech about myself, followed by a lecture about classroom rules and procedures. The first day went by without a hitch.

The problems began the following week when I attempted to make use of the classroom management theories and behavioral modification techniques that I'd learned in college. Not missing a beat, the students quickly discovered that I was not adequately prepared to handle them. This was because 85 percent of the textbook theories had no real life applications and did not take into account the cultural differences between African American students and their White counterparts.

As a new teacher, I was reluctant to ask my teacher-mentor, Mrs. Christmas, for help. To my surprise, she enthusiastically offered a lot of sound advice and a multitude of tips. In addition to seeking the expertise of my mentor, I began to watch how Mrs. Reese, a fellow fifth grade teacher and a veteran of our district, ran her classroom. The students who gave me problems were perfect angels in her class. She was confident, poised, and an excellent disciplinarian. Her students knew exactly what was expected of them at all times, and I longed to be like her.

Determined to make a difference in the lives of minority children, I spent my summer studying and researching strategies for educating African American youth. By the following fall, my teaching delivery had greatly improved, and I had become one of the strongest disciplinarians at my school. My colleagues frequently commented on how well behaved my students were. I owed a great deal of my success to believing that all youth, regardless of their backgrounds, can learn. I began writing the techniques that I had discovered into a notebook for future reference; by the end of my third year, I discovered that I had the basis for a really good book. Although I had been employing these techniques and discoveries in my classroom for three years, I had neither empirical evidence to prove that they actually worked nor the time to conduct research studies. I began to compile and review the literature of authors and researchers who corroborated my research. This book is the end result.

CHAPTER 1:
THE FACTORS AND STATISTICS

"Success is to be measured not so much by the position that one has reached in life as by the obstacles which he has overcome while trying to succeed."
Booker T. Washington, African American educator (1856–1915)

During the 1970s, concern grew in the African American community about how children were being processed through the American educational system. The perspective of Carter G. Woodson (1933) was rediscovered. He wrote that Black people have been "miseducated" into confusing their interests with those of the dominant society. Black people needed to maintain a clear identity of themselves as an oppressed people if they were going to be able to make a contribution to the struggle for liberation. Woodson wrote that the struggle for liberation is long-term; therefore, the educational system must serve a consciousness-raising function that will prepare Black people to make a contribution to a struggle that began centuries before they were born and that will extend centuries after their deaths (Hale, 1982, p. 2).

Although the civil rights movement fought for equal treatment under the law and equal educational opportunities, institutional racism has always found a way to circumvent its impact. The educational system must realize that the Black child is constantly bombarded with racial stereotypes and unfair assumptions that manifest themselves in the form of self-fulfilling

prophecies. Some White, Latino, Asian, and even African American teachers perpetuate theories of Black intellectual inferiority (consciously and subconsciously) by treating the Black child as though she is incapable of academic success. African American children don't need to be treated differently than their White counterparts; however, it is important for the educational system to recognize the cultural differences that exist between them in order for African American students to thrive academically.
Culture matters.

Institutional Racism

Historically, African American people have always valued education. Before the Emancipation Proclamation, it was unlawful to teach a slave to read and write, and sometimes the wages of disobedience was death. But did this stop slaves like Frederick Douglass from attempting to learn to read and write? No. Douglass convinced his slave master's wife and neighborhood children to teach him to read and write, and eventually he became a noted intellectual and abolitionist.

Boykin (1986) postulates that hegemony stemming from oppression and intellectual subjugation is a major problem in American schools. Boykin states that White and Black school authorities manifest this cycle of racism and oppression through their actions and demeanor toward Black students. When White values are juxtaposed against African American values, White authorities perceive their own as superior. Blacks are routinely sifted and placed into menial career paths that do not involve intellective competence. These actions perpetuate the myth of the intellectual superiority of the Eurocentric majority.

The Factors and Statistics

Back in the days of segregation, we were told by Black educational leaders that we would have to be twice as good as Whites and that we must be prepared to deal with racism and bigotry. We were also taught that we could fight back by being excellent and beyond reproach in all our endeavors. Today, unfortunately, the numbers of African American teachers, who were the traditional conveyors of that message, especially at the elementary school level, have dwindled considerably. The current generation of African American teachers no longer sees advocacy, role modeling, and surrogate parenting as part of their job description.

Teachers need to realize that at home, in their neighborhoods, and in school, many African American students face difficulties that can interfere with learning. Compared to their middle-class counterparts, it is true that disenfranchised students are more likely to be exposed to safety and health risks and less likely to receive regular medical care. They're more likely to be victims of crime. They're less likely to attend schools that have talented and gifted programs and are more likely to be identified as learning or emotionally disabled and placed in Exceptional Education. African American children need caring adults who will mentor them during turbulent times and not give up on them.

During my second year of teaching, I had a young man in my class who would always get into fights. He had been held back twice. Because of that, he was older than the rest of the class. Through my many talks with him, I quickly picked up on why he behaved the way he did. He thought that asserting himself physically was the way males were supposed to act when they felt threatened. He was the product of a single-parent household and rarely saw his dad. This young man was trying to become a strong Black man by mimicking what he saw other Black males doing in his

3

neighborhood and on TV. This led me to think about how it would feel to be a kid whose father rarely came around, who desperately needed guidance but had no one to turn to, and who was constantly being punished when he asserted his masculinity.

When I went home that night, I thought about what I could do to curb his aggressive tendencies and help him become a better student. I got to school the next day and put my plan into action. While taking steps to avoid alienating him from his friends, I set out to become his much-needed mentor. During my planning period, he and I would sit around and talk about how his life was going. I worked with him on his conflict resolution skills, etiquette, and academics, and before long he was showing marked improvement. I also checked in with his other teachers to see how he was doing in their classes. Over time, his grades improved, his office referrals decreased, and he became one of my best students. Due to his leadership status among his peers, an added bonus was that their behavior and academic performance improved, too. Along with becoming attached to this student, my work with him was also the basis for the formation of Project E.P.I.P.H.A.N.Y. (Envisioning Positive Innovative People Helping and Nurturing Youth).

Although this young man's problems were caused primarily by the lack of a male role model, there are several other factors that can interfere with an African American student's successful matriculation through today's educational system.

Self Sabotage
Many African American students believe that the American Dream was not meant for them (and to a certain extent they are

right). Boykin (1986) says that Black parents teach their children to strive for the American Dream and adhere to mundane constructs, but they also teach them to be careful and vigilant when dealing with "whites," "sambos," and "decent negroes" who serve as puppets for the White establishment. This perpetuates cultural dissension and an atmosphere of mistrust.

Family Influences

In the United States today, more than 63 percent of African American children come from single parent homes, most of which have the mother as the primary caregiver. Having no positive male role model, the boys in the home are particularly at risk to fail in school and get into trouble. As the mother's time is stretched so thinly, the girls in the family are at risk for teenage pregnancy. Many single parents have raised successful sons and daughters, but due to time and financial constraints on a single parent household, it is often difficult for the children to get the care and attention they need. As a disclaimer, I wholeheartedly believe that a Black woman can successfully raise an African American male on her own, but why should she have to complete such an assiduous task by herself?

Low Socioeconomic Status

African American children, unlike their White counterparts, have a greater probability of coming from a family with an income at or below the poverty level. They tend to live in poorer neighborhoods that provide fewer resources for learning and even fewer role models of educational and economic success. Children in such environments are led to believe that no other way of life may be possible for them. Furthermore, they may be alienated by peers who enjoy a higher economic status, who live in better neighborhoods, have newer clothes, computers, etc.

A form of intraracial segregation exists between the "haves" and the "have-nots" in African American high schools. The kids who wear the fancy clothes, drive the nice cars, and come from middle-class families are traditionally the most popular. Instead of trying to help their fellow brothers and sisters who are less fortunate, the haves ridicule the have-nots for not dressing extravagantly, wearing makeup, or having salon hairdos.

In addition, African American children from low-income backgrounds are expected to exhibit behavioral problems and academic failure. This expectation often becomes a self-fulfilling prophecy for these children.

In his book, *Family Life and School Achievement*, Reginald Clark looks at how income (low versus high) and parents (single versus two) relate to academic achievement. He found that success in school depends more on the quality of parental interaction than on economic factors or the number of parents in the household.

Parents of high-achieving children do five things consistently.

1.   Parents transmit hope. They say, "Life may not be all I want it to be, but it's going to be better for my children." They *believe* the world is going to be better for their children. Conversely, in some homes in which the parents feel downtrodden, a dismal attitude is transmitted to children. I am the product of a positive household. Although my father became disabled when I was four, he did not let his

predicament hold him down; he always remained optimistic. He taught me that education was the key to success and with it no man could ever hold me in the dismal mediocrity of mental peonage.

2.   Parents are consistent. In low-achieving homes, Mom has one rule on Monday and another rule on Wednesday. In high-achieving families, parents create and implement rules that remain unchanged from day to day.

3.   Parents are complimentary. In low-achieving homes, every other word has four letters, and insulting children is normal. Parents of high-achievers praise their children because they are sensitive about the effect their words will have.

4.   Parents have high expectations of their children. They expect them to do well and go on to college. They give clear messages about what's expected of them in the future.

5.   Parents believe they are the primary educators of their children. They do not put the major burden on the teacher but on themselves (Clark, 1983, as cited in Kunjufu, 1997).

Failing Schools

Unfortunately, failing schools go hand in hand with life in poor neighborhoods. These schools do not have the resources to compete with affluent areas that have more money for books, computers, salaries, etc. As a result, poorer schools have difficulty attracting well-trained teachers and administrators. Students in such situations may be written off, forgotten, or simply passed from grade to grade. Those who do stay around to graduate are generally ill prepared for college or the working world.

Research supports a correlation between academic failure and behavioral problems among African American children (as well as White children). For example, a negative relationship was found between delinquency and school achievement; that is, as school achievement decreased, delinquency increased (Tucker, 1999).

Cultural Gaps

The uniqueness of African American culture sets it apart from White cultures and consequently is often viewed as negative. African American hairstyles, dress, music, body language, and verbal communication styles can be disconcerting to a society that is based on conformity.

When defining or identifying behavioral problems among a group of children, it is important to consider the influence of culture on the definition and perception of the behaviors. For example, when African American teen males aggressively argue with each other in an intimidating manner, teachers who do not understand African American culture may label their behavior as fighting when actually the teens are verbally "woofing" or relieving tension to avoid fighting. Woofing is a common practice among African American teens. Without a rule against it or understanding of it, this behavior would be labeled fighting and incorrectly considered a behavioral problem (Tucker, 1999).

Certain behaviors and language that are acceptable within the African American community may be considered highly racist outside of the community, such as the use of the term "nigga." Educators should learn about such differences so that they appropriately temper their responses to students and not alienate them by disciplining behaviors that are a part of the culture.

The Factors and Statistics

Regarding the word "nigga," African American youth (in my mind) have done something that educated scholars could not. By redefining "nigga" as a term of endearment, they have effectively deconstructed this derogatory term ("nigga," undesirable), defined its perceived opposite (White, "virtuous"), and concluded that Blacks and Whites are not inherently different. With one word they have consciously and subconsciously destroyed the hierarchy of race and White supremacy.

Another area where significant cultural gaps can exist is in the area of speech. Ebonics, as it is often called, is a type of African American speech that can lead others to believe that those who speak it are unintelligent. Of course this isn't true in many cases, but this perception can result in such individuals being written off by educators, as well by as employers.

Interestingly, students themselves know the good teachers from the bad ones. The staff knows who's a good teacher and who isn't, and so, of course, do administrators. Some teachers are racist, and they do not bond with students from different social and economic backgrounds. This cannot help but impact academic achievement. We need strong administrators who will hold poor teachers accountable and make it uncomfortable for them to stay in the classroom. We need parents who, when their children tell them they have a poor teacher, recognize that's unacceptable and do something about it. Teachers must begin to police themselves and hold each other accountable (Kunjufu, 1997).

Crime and Drug Abuse

It is no secret that the majority of those incarcerated in the nation's prisons are primarily young African Americans males. We may think that law enforcement has a racial bias, but the fact is that the stage is set long before the handcuffs ever go on.

Drug abuse and the commission of crimes are the all-too-frequent outcomes of the inability of young people to overcome the risk factors of single-parent homes, poverty, failing schools, and cultural gaps. As vulnerable young people begin to feel confused and alienated by the world around them, they seek physical and emotional control in the only ways they believe are available to them—through drug use and crime.

In his book, *Critical Issues in Educating African American Youth*, Dr. Jawanza Kunjufu describes an encounter with a 19-year-old youth. This youth told Dr. Kunjufu that he would rather die at 21 years old if it meant he could have at least two years of driving a BMW (even if he had to sell drugs) than work 65 years in a slave job with no car. He understood Kunjufu's position about valuing life and reaping benefits in the long-term, and he acknowledged the possibility that he could do well at school and have a successful career. However, he believed he had a better chance of owning a BMW through the sale of drugs than an education.

According to Kunjufu, the question of motivation as it relates to academic achievement has new meaning for today's kids. Parents tell their children that they should want a good education and a career that will make them money, but children are becoming increasingly skeptical about this point of view. They are asking questions such as, "Work hard for whom?" and "Get a good education for what?" They want to be employers, not employees. They have no desire to end up on welfare or work at McDonald's. Children watch adults who have a good education working a JOB, and this is not attractive to them. Our children have found plenty of other ways to make money that don't require a good education.

They believe they can make more money—faster money—in drugs and other crimes, sports, music, and the lottery. These five areas compete with the traditional educational approach, and they capture children's attention and imagination in the short term.

Educators must show children that there are better odds in the academic arena than in drugs, sports, crime, music, and the lottery. For example, our children see drug winners, but rarely do they see drug losers. We need to take them to prisons, drug abuse programs, hospitals, and cemeteries. Have them list all the people they know who have been selling drugs for five years and report their current status. We must show them the mathematical odds of making it in the NBA: 1,000,000 to one (Kunjufu, 1989).

While the ongoing effects of segregation have taken its toll on the overall educational outcomes for African American students, a number of other factors affect the educational results for this student population as well.

Lack of African American Teachers

When school systems were officially segregated, Black children attended schools that were run mostly by experienced Black educators. These teachers and administrators were actually better qualified and more experienced than their White counterparts (Southern Education Reporting Service, 1959). However, with the end of segregation came substantial layoffs. In 17 states, 38,000 African Americans lost their jobs as teachers and administrators between 1954 and 1965 (King, 1993). The state of education for Black youth has not been the same since. In 1995, African American teachers made up only 7.3 percent of the teaching force in public schools (National Education Association, 1997).

African American teachers are vital in the lives of Black children because they often play the role of missing parental figures by acting as disciplinarians, counselors, and role models. According to one study, low-achieving African American students benefit most from relationships with experienced African American teachers (King, 1993). African American teachers also tend not to place blame on families or society for student failure (Foster, 1990).

Young African American students can directly benefit from relationships with young African American teachers 23–35 because these teachers often serve as surrogate big brothers and sisters and are cognizant of the latest trends in music, sports, fashion, etc. They also empathize with the X generation's sense of situated identity conflict and inadequacy.

Resistance to Middle-Class School Norms

Instead of surrendering to the typical standards of a school environment which many African American students view as cruel and oppressive, some students end up rejecting European American speech patterns and devaluing high academic achievement, therefore unintentionally limiting themselves (King, 1993; Gobo, 1990). On the other hand, there are African American students who respond in the opposite way. These high-achieving students cite their awareness of racism and prejudice as a motivation to do extremely well, thus preparing themselves to fight these evils (King, 1993). I applaud the fact that many of our African American males refuse to assimilate into the dominant culture, but sometimes it may be better to play the game. This does not mean becoming a sellout or the "Decent Negro" that Nas talks about on his latest album, *Streets Disciple*; it means that you are a very sagacious individual.

Lack of Priorities

Let's do a little role playing. Pretend you are a 15-year-old African American teenager and you have one of two choices: watch BET (Black Entertainment Television) or do your homework. The typical African American will probably decide to watch television and do homework later, but it never seems to get done, does it? If you have your priorities in order, you will probably do your homework first and watch TV later. Then your homework is complete and you get a chance to watch 106 & Park.

Unfortunately, many African American children do not realize that school should be their first priority. I can personally attest to this because in high school, homework was not even my #2 priority. Eventually I woke up and began to take my schoolwork seriously.

Low Teacher Expectations

African American children are especially susceptible to teacher expectations. Teacher expectations, even when based on erroneous information, can influence the academic performance of children. In today's society, according to Janice Hale-Benson, when African American children exhibit poor reading skills, psychologists say it is because the children have inferior cognitive capabilities or do not value education. When White middle-class children exhibit poor reading skills, it is seldom suggested that they are unable to learn or that they are deficient in any way. Psychologists generally say that the problem is in the method of instruction or inappropriate matches between curriculum and the child's level of development. These are blatant examples of the effect of institutional racism on student assessment and expectations. And as we know, low expectations for African American students become self-fulfilling prophecies.

Low Effort Syndrome

This phrase was coined by Jonathon Ogbu in his monumental book, *Black American Students in an Affluent Suburb*. It simply means that some African American pupils are not adequately engaged in their academic endeavors. The time that most African American children spend actively engaged in learning, studying, and enrichment is not conducive to the acquisition of intellective competence and perpetuates the myth of African American intellectual inferiority. In layman's terms, most African American students do not work hard in school. As Ogbu was conducting his ethnographic research, some African American students disclosed that they do not work as hard as they should and could. They did just enough to get by. This phenomenon can be attributed to mixed-up priorities, peer pressure, and a lack of parental involvement.

Anti-Intellectualism

In *Losing the Race: Self Sabotage in Black America*, John McWorther chronicles the trend of anti-intellectualism in Black

America. He argues that although Black children are not banned from doing well in school, they are culturally conditioned to exacerbate a "cult of victimology." This phenomenon leads many scholars to aim solutions at victimhood rather than admit that this problem of poor academic performance is a cultural norm. In my opinion, anti-intellectualism is one of the most pernicious factors that contribute to the achievement gap.

Social Services

In order to effectively assist African American students, the majority of social services should be placed within the school system. This would provide schools with the resources needed to alleviate a broad spectrum of problems. It also would provide valuable resources for African American children and their parents, and provide a support system capable of addressing their problems and creating solutions that have long-term viability.

Social welfare is not a free handout. It is a necessary component in a society that has a track record of discriminating against its neediest members. Everyone should be afforded the opportunity to better themselves and sometimes they need a little help.

The Statistics

Black children are less likely than White or Hispanic children to live in a married-couple family. In 2000, 37 percent of Black children under 18 lived in two-parent families, and 53 percent lived in single-parent families. This percentage of Black children living in two-parent families is lower than the percentage for White and Hispanic children (78 percent and 65 percent, respectively). Black children under 18 are much more likely to live with only their mother (49 percent) than with only their father (4 percent).

31 percent of Black children lived in poverty in 2000. This percentage is higher than both the percentage of White children (9 percent) and the percentage of Hispanic children (28 percent) living below the poverty level. No differences were detected between the percent of Hispanic families and the percent of Black families living below the poverty level, which was both higher than their counterpart, White families. The percentage of Black female-headed households below the poverty level in 2000 was nearly 6 times higher than the percentage of Black married-couple households below the poverty level. Thirty-five percent of all Black female-headed households were below the poverty level in 2000, whereas 6 percent of all married-couple Black families were below the poverty level.

In 2000, 22 percent of Black 8th-graders and 29 percent of Black 12th-graders were absent 3 or more days in the previous month.

In 1999, 18 percent of Black students in kindergarten through 12th grade had ever repeated at least one grade. Racial/ethnic differences also were evident in suspension and expulsion rates. In 1999, 35 percent of Black students in grades 7 through 12 had been suspended or expelled at some point in their school careers, higher than the 20 percent of Hispanics and 15 percent of Whites.

In 2000, 13 percent of Black 16- to 24-year-olds had not earned a high school credential.

The Factors and Statistics

Black kindergartners are less likely than their White and Asian peers to persist at tasks, to be eager to learn, and to pay attention according to their teachers." "In 1999, 9-year-old Black students had an average NAEP mathematics scale score lower than the score for White 9-year-olds.

Despite gains among Black students at all three age groups since the 1970s, their academic performance in 1999 remained statistically significantly lower than that of White students.

In 2001, Black students scored lower than all other racial groups and Hispanic subgroups on both the verbal and the mathematics section of the SAT. On average, Black students scored 96 points lower than White students on the verbal section in 2001, and they scored 105 points lower than White students on the mathematics section in the same year.

The average composite score for Blacks on the ACT in 2001 was 16.9, lower than the other racial/ethnic groups' average composite scores and lower than the threshold indicator of college preparedness.

In 1998, 71 percent of entering kindergartners from Black or Hispanic families had one or more risk factors, compared to 29 percent of those from White families and 61 percent from Asian families.

In 2001, Black students generally were less likely to use computers at school than White students but more likely than Hispanic students to do so.

Black females were nearly two-thirds (63 percent) of the Black enrollment in colleges and universities in 2000. In 2000, Blacks ages 25 and over were more likely than Hispanics but less likely than Whites to have earned an associate, bachelor's or master's degree. Also, Black adults were less likely to receive first professional and doctor's degrees than White adults.

CHAPTER 2:
ROLE CALL: WHO'S ACCOUNTABLE?

"The educational system of a country is worthless unless it [revolutionizes the social order]. Men of scholarship, and prophetic insight, must show us the right way and lead us into light which is shining brighter and brighter."
Carter G. Woodson, African American historian and educator (1875–1950)

Joseph is a 13 year-old Black male who is highly intelligent but has had problems controlling his temper. When I first initiated his case study, Joseph was a fifth grade student with severe anger management issues and sociopathic tendencies. As I served as his Social Studies instructor during the 2002–2003 school year, I had first-hand knowledge of 65 percent of Joseph's tirades and had to intervene during several of his successful and attempted assaults on his peers. By the end of the school term, Joseph's GPA was 2.2, and he had accumulated 35 office referrals. At the beginning of the 2003–2004 school term, I started Project E.P.I.P.H.A.N.Y. (Envisioning Positive Innovative People Helping and Nurturing Youth), a school-based mentoring program serving Hazlehurst Middle School. I referred Joseph to my program because I believed that he could benefit from a mentoring relationship with a professional male.

Joseph is the product of a two-parent household. His father was a former factory worker who became disabled after a heart attack. Prior to his heart attack, Joseph's father was the alpha male and head of the house. When his physical capacity became severely limited, Joseph was given the responsibility of being his father's hands and legs.

Although Joseph was in regular fifth grade classes, he was constantly getting into fights and skirmishes. Despite his above average intelligence, Joseph was failing three of his courses and barely passing the other two. During our initial talk, Joseph was cooperative. I asked him if he would like to participate in the mentoring program, and he said yes. During the interview I gave Joseph a sentence completion test. Examples of his responses to several of the incomplete sentences are as follows (Joseph's answers are italicized):

1. I can't understand why *I have so many responsibilities.*
2. I often wish *that my dad wasn't sick.*
3. I hate *to hear people say bad things about me.*
4. I get mad *when kids tease me.*

After our interview I developed a course of action I call cognitive restructuring. I believe that in order to change the negative behavior of African American males, we must first identify and understand the social, emotional, and educational forces that have contributed to their present level of functioning. We then need to pinpoint how and why these forces have molded the misconceptions that a child believes to be true.

The concept of cognitive restructuring was inspired by Albert Ellis's Rational Emotive Therapy. Ellis discloses that life events are not responsible for the emotions that we experience but our perceptions and reactions to these events. For example, a teenage child may say, "It's my fault that my father abandoned me. I must have done something to drive him away." These sentiments are likely to facilitate feelings of sadness and self-hatred. Helping a child understand that his father abandoned him for his own reasons, not because of anything the child did, is the first step in cognitive restructuring.

Cognitive restructuring takes Ellis's theory a step further. At the beginning of the treatment, each child is paired with a mentor. The mentor serves as a positive role model, teaching the child to take a proactive approach to life. Being proactive means that the child is responsible for her own happiness or unhappiness. Becoming proactive allows the child to enlarge her circle of control. As children make pro-activity a way of life, they gradually become free of the constraints of anger and guilt.

I served as Joseph's mentor during this process, and after undergoing cognitive restructuring, Joseph's referrals decreased from 30 the previous year, to one this year. His GPA increased from a 2.2 to a 3.1. These results clearly illustrate that cognitive restructuring had a dramatic effect on Joseph's behavior and GPA.

Joseph was a young man who, though facing many hardships in his life, ultimately transcended his conditioning to become a success. When children like Joseph cry out for help by failing academically or acting out, who is responsible for African American students falling through the cracks? If you ask teachers, the parents are to blame. If you ask the parents, teachers are to blame. If you ask administrators, the fault lies with the lack of parental involvement and quality teachers. If you ask the community, schools are to blame. The truth is that it is everyone's job to effectively guide African American students through their formative years to adulthood. If we do not nurture and cultivate the next generation of Black leaders, who will uphold our legacy?

21

The Role of Self-Esteem

The nature of esteem is core to understanding these factors and how they relate to at-risk youth. According to Dr. Kunjufu, many different forms of esteem exist besides self-esteem, including peer, parent, spouse, career, material, and physical esteem, just to name a few. For example, low physical esteem results when people do not feel good about themselves. Their self-worth is dependent on their physical health and appearance, especially their weight. Gaining 25 pounds results in lowered physical esteem. Suffering from a disease or illness can also affect self-esteem.

For others, esteem is based on material possessions. For many people, self-worth is based on their cars or clothes. In low-income areas, there are often finer cars parked near the projects than there are in affluent suburbs. Secretaries who work downtown and make under $10,000 out-dress their bosses who make more than $60,000. These people measure their worth by their possessions.

Other sources of esteem include careers, jobs, and degrees. We say, "I've got a B.A., an M.A., and a Ph.D. I'm vice president in charge of the ...." A significant other, or lack thereof, can also be a source of esteem.

Parent esteem is another important factor. Many parents try to live their lives through their children, and many adults are still trying to please their parents. It is difficult to feel good about yourself when you're trying to please someone else.

Parents must understand how their words affect their children. Often we only look at physical abuse, but one study looking at parents' statements found that of the 314 statements made to children, 296 were negative. These parents love their children but say damaging things to them—things their children will never forget no matter how many material gifts are given.

Peer pressure is a significant issue as well, and good parents have found ways to monitor its effects. First, these parents know who their children's friends are. Second, they invite their children's friends over so they can get to know them better. Finally, they have their children regularly contact them so they can keep tabs on their activities, sometimes every hour on the hour. And it's not that kids can't deal drugs or get pregnant in an hour, but it makes it a lot more difficult.

Parents and teachers can do all the right things and still, children will get into trouble. This can often be caused by the child's friends who are more concerned about what kind of gym shoes and clothes they wear, how well they dance, fight, and play basketball, rather than concentrating on doing well in school.

In order to successfully combat peer pressure, a high level of self-esteem is vitally important. Kunjufu believes that the factors that help develop self-esteem are: a relationship with God, unconditional love from parents, high expectations from teachers, racial or ethnic pride, identifying talents and previous accomplishments, and for young people, college and career plans. When self-esteem is high and when children receive proper motivation, they achieve academically (Kunjufu, 1997).

The Role of Parents

Parent participation plays a large role in a child's academic success. Faculty and staff must seek and secure involvement and form partnerships with parents if children are to succeed academically, especially since school occupies only nine percent of children's lives.

Unfortunately, in African American communities, parent participation in schools is often low, and there are several reasons why. First of all, the underlying issue of power must be explored. African American parents often feel they lack the ability to mobilize power and resources. These parents have few avenues by which they can challenge curriculum choices, instructional strategies, or course placement decisions. They report feeling isolated, alienated, disengaged, intimidated, and a host of other negative feelings about their interactions with school personnel. Overwhelmingly, they are treated like second-class citizens, and they frequently respond by withdrawing.

Instead of criticizing what they are doing wrong, African American parents, like all parents, need support and encouragement to continue what they are doing right. For example, the fact that many families exist within an extended household or in family kinship networks should be viewed as a strength, not a weakness. Schools can improve the academic achievement of African American children, and all children, when they work in partnership with parents. Students improve when their families are continually involved and emphasize the importance of schooling. Relying on the ideas of experts and ignoring the real people—the families—is a mistake. Academic achievement is a function of schools, parents, and students operating in harmony toward the pursuit of a common goal (Obiakor & Ford, 2002, p.153–4).

The Role of Schools
While African American students' motivation must be cultivated at home, one of the most effective steps toward academic

improvement is a positive school environment. Schools can increase student motivation by implementing policies that promote the following:
- Goal setting and self-regulation
- Student choices
- Student achievements
- Teamwork and cooperative learning
- Self-assessment models rather than social comparisons.

In addition, teachers can enhance students' personal motivation by allowing them to feel in control of their own learning.

Unfortunately, not all schools implement policies that promote the self. There are several factors that affect an African American student's ability to reach his or her potential, especially in schools that are located within large, urban school districts. Teachers often form perceptions and judgments about students based on race, data found in personal records, and the environments in which they live. For example, a White student from an affluent area of town may be perceived as smart and well behaved, while an African American student coming from the poorest area of town may be viewed having behavioral problems and not smart. Such perceptions put unnecessary burdens on how African American students view their abilities and self-concepts.

Teachers often form preliminary expectations and assign hasty labels to students based on their body shape, gender, race, ethnicity, name, attractiveness, dialect, and socioeconomic level. A teacher who perceives a student as smart will expect more work from the child. On the other hand, a teacher who perceives a student as not smart will expect less from the child. Students who are perceived as low in ability are rarely given opportunities to learn new materials—they are called on less in class, get little praise, and are provided less informative feedback. Embedded in such perceptions is the belief that poor students cannot do well in school because they lack the ability. Such beliefs are absorbed within students and contribute to the inaccurate self-knowledge, self-esteem, and self-ideal they form of themselves. Teacher expectations usually lead to self-fulfilling tendencies among students. Therefore, teachers are encouraged to assess their own attitudes, beliefs, and expectations as they work with African American students (Obiakor & Ford, 2002, p. 124–5).

Modern classrooms tend to be based on a Eurocentric worldview. When an African American student does not perform according to this Eurocentric worldview, his resistance to assimilation is dealt with harshly. When cultural conflicts play out in the classroom setting, African American children are unjustly persecuted for not being the typical Eurocentric child or at least willing to cross over. Teachers can combat the aforementioned practices by employing culturally responsive instruction. A culturally responsive classroom is a much better place for all students, as African American and all minority children are given the opportunity to truly thrive academically.

The Role of Teachers

It is at this point in the book that I find it necessary to pay homage to some of the influential teachers in my life.

Mr. Verna Joe Nelson first comes to mind. He was my seventh and tenth grade History teacher who made Social Studies come alive, telling us stories of our past and how it had been distorted by historians. We learned about slavery and how it was replaced by a comparably milder form of bondage, sharecropping. We learned about the civil rights movement and the prophesies of Martin Luther King.

Mr. Foster Topp helped shape my current political views. During my senior year, I had the pleasure of taking his American Government class. We learned about the various forms of government, but of course we focused on Democracy. His views on political theory have a permanent place in my mental rolodex.

Mrs. Sandra Miller sparked my initial love of literature during my junior year. I vividly remember reading *The Red Badge of Courage* and numerous other books while in her class, but she never knew about my love of reading. At school I seemed apathetic about my studies, but when I got home I would close the door to my room and read classic novels like *Roots* and *Uncle Tom's Cabin*. I had a voracious appetite for knowledge, but I never displayed or cultivated it.

Mrs. Katie Ruth Walker, my freshman and senior year English teacher, turned me on to Chaucer, Baldwin, Hughes, Shakespeare, and T. S. Elliot—inadvertently. She also never knew about my love for reading. I remember having the option of reciting the Prologue to the *Canterbury Tales* in Standard English or Old English and choosing to pontificate in Old English just to impress her.

Teachers are important to the success of all students. African American children often view teachers as mentors and role models in their lives. Through their actions, teachers send messages to children about whether they are accepted and competent enough to accomplish tasks given and about whether they are true members of the learning community.

Shade, Kelly, and Oberg (1998) assert that teachers must set a stage and climate for learning that stimulate interest within the child. Teachers send verbal and nonverbal messages to students that indicate their capabilities for success, and establish the pace and level of intellectual stimulation in the classroom. Through their choice of learning activities, as well as how they present them, teachers must strive to provide instruction that will be effective for students using a variety of learning styles.

According to the researchers, the following seven principles are crucial in the establishment of a culturally responsive learning environment:

1. Teachers are personally inviting.
2. Classroom is physically inviting.
3. Students are rewarded for their academic successes.
4. Changes are made to accommodate cultural differences.
5. Classroom is managed with firm, consistent, loving control.
6. Interactions stress cooperation rather than individuality.

A major role of teachers is to help students learn success behaviors and adaptive skills as a means of preventing behavioral problems. Yet, because of the many responsibilities teachers have (e.g., teaching basic course work, correcting homework, keeping records, and attending teacher meetings), they often don't have the time to develop these skills in their students. However, teachers can significantly impact the occurrence of these behaviors and skills, even in the little time they have.

Success behaviors are those that contribute to a positive self-presentation and are typically used to get and keep a job and to take advantage of opportunities in life. These behaviors include maintaining eye contact, studying and preparing for class, listening while others are talking, using good manners, asking questions about what is not understood, using complete sentences, and following instructions. Teachers should make and post a list of success behaviors, review and discuss the list with all of their students, review and discuss the list individually with African American students, and then praise the occurrence of these behaviors (Tucker, 1999, p. 186).

Teaching African American children adaptive skills, including communication skills (e.g., how to express feelings, make a complete sentence, and write a business letter), socialization skills (e.g., how to resolve conflict, problem solve, initiate a conversation, and interview for a job), and daily living skills (e.g., how to write a check and balance a checkbook, make an emergency telephone call, pay bills), is something that most teachers agree is important. Yet, many teachers feel that these skills should be taught at home.

The problem is that neither parents nor teachers are sure how to teach these skills. Furthermore, many educators feel it is hard enough to teach math, reading, science, history, and other courses without adding adaptive skills. However, if teachers don't teach these skills, many African American students won't learn them. Learning adaptive skills is important for social, academic, and life success, all three of which are the main deterrents of behavioral problems.

One thing that teachers can do to teach these skills is to integrate them into their teaching of academics. For example, when teaching math, the math assignment could be to calculate the cost of a list of grocery items, and then write a check to pay for them. This assignment adds interest to the task, and also prepares them for something students will do in real life. Fortunately, there is a growing recognition in schools that what is taught in the classroom needs to be directly related to what students will do in the real world to be successful in life.

Teachers can also help students learn adaptive skills during field trips in which they learn by doing. They can learn about banking, saving money, check writing, etc., by taking a field trip to the bank. Bank professionals can teach students the adaptive skills related to their profession. Through this process, some students might decide on a banking career as opposed to becoming a school dropout. The bank could then provide mentors to work with students interested in the banking field.

Another creative way teachers can help children learn adaptive skills is by inviting experts in various fields to teach these skills in the classroom, thereby teaching and serving as a role model at the same time (Tucker, 1999, p. 186–187).

The Role of Administrators

Effective school administrators emphasize the acquisition of basic skills and are actively involved in the development of multicultural curricula that foster cross-cultural understanding. They support staff by listening to suggestions and being empathetic to their complaints. They are effective in maintaining discipline and order in the school building.

Dr. Brown was the principal of Hazlehurst Elementary School (PreK–fourth grade) while I was at Hazlehurst Upper Elementary/Middle/Junior High School (fifth–eighth grades). Both schools were really one school, the Hazlehurst Middle School.

Dr. Brown understood the importance of effective leadership in the school building and how it dictates school climate. His leadership style can be best described as supportive. Dr. Brown let his employees know exactly what they were expected to do, but he also considered their needs, showed concern for their welfare, and created a friendly working environment. He always encouraged his staff and students to be the best they could be. He will never know what his periodic words of encouragement meant to me, and I wish I would have had the pleasure of directly benefiting from his knowledge base.

His vision resulted in excellent student achievement. Every summer, when the MCT (Mississippi Curriculum Test) results were released, his kids always performed exceedingly well. He was the epitome of top level management, and his leadership style fostered an environment that was conducive to learning and student achievement.

Dr. Robinson was the Assistant Superintendent while I was at Hazlehurst Middle School. She was poised and intelligent, an effective leader. She always encouraged me to strive to be best educator I could be. She really loved her job and believed in our students and staff. It is this type of leadership that was responsible for Hazlehurst City Schools' excellent test scores during the 2003–2004 school years. I remember running into Dr. Robinson during summer break at a restaurant. She sat with me and we talked about current issues in education. I told her about my dream of obtaining a doctorate in education. She encouraged me to pursue that dream and to never let go of it.

The late Robert McDaniel was one of the most influential administrators I have ever had the honor to know. He was poised, confident, and made me believe that my dreams really can come true. He was the first African American superintendent in the Hazlehurst City School District and was responsible for several innovative creations, most notably the current national bus

31

numbering system. His wife, Dr. Bettye McDaniel, gave me my first teaching job.

The Role of the Community

Like the family, the community plays a key role in the development of self-identity. African American communities are frequently viewed negatively by those who live in them and by outsiders who are ignorant of what happens there, but they may house a wealth of resources that African American students can access. In fact, all individuals should take advantage of the many learning opportunities that are available within their communities (i.e., libraries, museums, schools, jobs and entrepreneurial offers).

One of the most effective ways in which community establishments can help African American students develop self-confidence and mastery is by providing them with service learning opportunities. Service learning is a work-based learning experience in which students learn, develop, and apply academic and vocational skills to address the real-life needs of their local communities. Such experiences are designed to connect students to their community and give them opportunities to apply learned skills in real-life settings while helping them develop the attitudes, values, and behaviors that will lead them to become contributing members of society (Obiakor & Ford, 2002, p. 126–7).

Role Models

African American role models and mentors can be instrumental in providing consistent help and encouragement to

African American children who do not otherwise receive such support. According to Ascher (1992), the flight of middle-class African Americans from inner-city neighborhoods and the incidence of high unemployment among those who remain have resulted in a lack of appropriate mainstream role models in inner-city homes, communities, and media. Furthermore, Ascher (1992) calls attention to the fact that only 1.2 percent of all teachers are African American men. Many adults feel they are too busy to be role models and mentors for African American children, as they are consumed with trying to hold on to their middle-class status and/or fighting racism and discrimination via various projects and organizations.

Interventions designed to modify and prevent behavioral problems and academic failure would be more successful if individuals, especially males, committed to consistently giving children encouragement and help. Mentors and role models don't have to speak perfect English, have prestigious jobs, or be successful as traditionally defined. They don't even have to be African American. The most important thing is that these people are respected in their communities and are committed to helping at-risk children reach their full potential (Tucker, 1999, p. 20).

Goal Setting

African American students, like all students, need well-defined goals. More importantly, they need to see a direct relationship between doing well in school and achieving those goals.

Most parents, grandparents, and other adult family members passionately tell youth how important it is for them to be "somebody." They also passionately tell them what they *don't* want them to be. For example, in interviews with African American grandmothers, Hale-Benson (1986) found that these women did not want their grandchildren to do hard labor, menial jobs, or domestic work.

Many African American children, especially those from low socioeconomic backgrounds, grow up feeling the need to be successful without having a destination or the tools to reach that destination. In other words, these children do not have short-term academic goals (e.g., to successfully pass first grade, to graduate from junior high school) or long-term career goals (e.g., to become a civil rights lawyer). Children who do have clearly defined goals are often at a loss as to how to attain them.

Goals are important in developing self-motivation, which promotes and sustains behaviors such as studying, doing homework, etc. Children will usually expend a lot of time and energy doing things when they know there is a direct connection between what they want and the time and energy it takes to get it.

That's why it's important that children be taught the connection between doing well in biology and becoming a doctor or nurse, for example. It doesn't take a lot of effort to arrange for a doctor or nurse to visit a school to talk to children about the importance of studying science, having self-discipline, and speaking Standard English as they pursue a medical career. It's also simple to arrange to visit a hospital or clinic to talk to the staff and see how they work.

It's no mystery that the number of college students pursuing careers in criminal justice and forensics has skyrocketed since the popular show *CSI* aired on television. Young people see a career that appears interesting to them, and they actively pursue it.

Therefore, it's vital that schools, parents, and community leaders work together to ensure that the education of African American children, and all children, includes:
1. Identifying long-term career or job goals
2. Identifying short-term goals related to their long-term goals
3. Meeting African American adults in various jobs and careers
4. Participating in school and field trip experiences that will provide information related to their career goals.

Such educational experiences are particularly important for African American children; there are so many exciting and lucrative careers to which African American children will never be exposed without schools and community leaders providing this opportunity. Children need help in seeing the relationship between school success and career success. Once they understand the connection, their self-motivation to learn and achieve is enhanced (Tucker, 1999, p. 20–21).

The idea that "it takes a village to raise a child" is a core part of my approach to educating African American children. Every stakeholder in the education of our children must assume their important roles in the war against discrimination and bigotry in our schools. African Americans, and all minorities, must come to the table to devise a viable plan. We must find a way to implement the experiences and culture of all races into curriculum and instruction in order to ensure that all children receive a quality education. No longer should a "one size fits all" approach to teaching be practiced or tolerated. Teachers, administrators, parents, and the community must be held accountable for the current state of America's educational system. No one is free from blame.

CHAPTER 3:
RESPONDING TO ACADEMIC FAILURE AND MISBEHAVIOR

"We have a powerful potential in our youth, and we must have the courage to change old ideas and practices so that we may direct their power toward good ends."
Mary McLeod Bethune, Educator/Founder, Bethune-Cookman College (1875–1955)

During my second year of teaching, I had a student in my Social Studies class who tried her best but just couldn't pass my quizzes or tests. She would complete her homework and participate in class, but to no avail.

My job was not to be complacent with her performance but to help lift her to the next level. I decided to try Gardner's Eight Multiple Intelligences. This student turned out to be an Interpersonal (leader) learner. She loved to work with her classmates on various tasks. To tap into this talent, I provided extra opportunities for her to work in cooperative learning groups, and she was usually elected the leader of any given group because of her keen interpersonal skills.

As a result, she began to succeed academically in my class and ended the semester with an A. Many factors aided her ascension into the next level of academic achievement, but the most important factor was the faith I had in her and the willingness to ensure that she succeeded academically and personally. Most students will do anything to live up to your faith in them, but they have to believe that your faith is genuine. Once she gained a little taste of confidence, there was no stopping her.

When Nothing Seems to Work

Although I was successful in helping this child overcome her behavioral problems, sometimes the answers are not so easy to find. Teachers must work with the unique learning needs of many children, not just one. We must determine if the problem is academic or behavioral, as well as factor in the parent's attitude regarding the issue at hand. Teachers will be more positive, supportive, and helpful with children whose parents are highly involved. Teachers also tend to be much more reactive to an African American child's behavioral problems than academic ones.

Teachers and Academic Failure

Teachers of African American children who are failing academically may respond by:

1. Reading the child's cumulative records to find out how family history/dynamics might be contributing to the child's academic failure and/or behavioral problems. Unfortunately, this information may be distorted if it was obtained by a teacher or administrator with a cultural and/or socioeconomic bias against the child.

2. Talking to colleagues who taught the child. If the consensus is that the child is not sufficiently motivated to learn and the parents are not invested in helping the child or are hostile toward teachers, then the child's failure may simply be accepted. This acceptance is especially likely if the child's current teacher decides that there is nothing more that can be done. If the teacher finds out that the child has been doing much better in other teachers' classes and thus concludes that

the problem is with him, this may cause feelings of guilt or resentment toward the child.

3. Blaming parents for the academic failure, especially if they don't attend parent-teacher conferences. While the teacher may give the child extra help, without additional outside tutoring, she may feel it's a waste of time.

4. Referring the child for assessment to determine if the child has a learning disorder, disability, or other problem that is causing the academic failure.

5. Feeling frustrated with the child when additional tutoring doesn't result in improved academic performance.

6. Giving up after having tried on several occasions and in several ways to help the child do better academically.

Teachers of African American children who exhibit behavioral problems may respond by:

1. Punishing the child for the inappropriate behaviors by withdrawing a privilege or imposing time-out periods. However, for many African American children, such separation only serves to reinforce any feelings of discrimination and associated resentment, even though the punishment has nothing to do with discrimination.

2. Sending the child to the principal's office, where the child is warned (often in the form of threats) of the potential consequences of his behavior. Regardless of the outcome, the child misses valuable class time, which in turn results in his getting progressively farther behind academically.

3. Requesting that the child be removed from the classroom and/ or suspended, often resulting in continued academic failure or mounting academic weaknesses.

Parents and Academic Failure

In response to their child's academic failure or behavioral problems, parents may react by:

1. Blaming themselves and past family problems for their child's issues. As a result, they may become tolerant of the child's academic failure and behavior. Children may use this tolerance as an excuse to give up.

2. Angrily accusing the child of trying to hurt them. In turn, the child responds in angry and resentful ways, consequently resisting any attempts to improve his academic performance or behavior.

3. Blaming the teacher for seeming to not care about the child or get them the help they need. They may also view the teachers' perceived lack of caring as racism. As a result, teachers may feel resentful, avoiding contact with the parents and thus limiting any chance for a team approach to address the child's issues and improve their chances for improvement and success.

4. Taking their child to a psychologist or counselor in the hope that they can "fix" the child's problem or recommend a strategy that will get the child to quickly become more academically inclined and behaviorally successful. However, parents can become frustrated with a therapist who spends more time identifying the problems than finding possible solutions.

5. Increasing the frequency and severity of punishments. As a result, the child can become even more determined to teach the parents that such punishments will not bring the results they want, no matter how harsh. The child may even begin to deliberately act out to hurt her parents.

6. Giving up trying to help, waiting instead for the child to come around on his own. However, parents continue to express their disappointment in the child's poor performance, and the dialogue becomes increasingly negative, critical, and eventually, reinforcing.

The aforementioned approaches by teachers and parents should be avoided at all costs.

Obviously, there are no easy answers about what to do when attempts to eliminate academic failure and behavioral problems have failed. It is vitally important that parents and teachers not give up on these children, no matter how daunting the challenge might be. However, sometimes it can be helpful for parents, educators, etc. to take a break and step back for a while so that they can evaluate the situation with a clear head. It is not uncommon for those involved to become so emotionally entangled in a situation as to lose their perspective about what is really important and what steps need to be taken to continue to assist the child.

To ensure success, parents with school-aged children should:

- Take some time everyday to focus on other aspects of their lives, such as friends, hobbies, education, etc. that don't involve thinking about the child's problems. Such a breather will help lessen any resentment they may feel toward the child and assist in preventing burnout.
- As often as possible, try to focus on what the child does well in school—either academically or behaviorally. It's easy to become so wrapped up in the problems of children that parents may overlook their wonderful qualities and the things they do right every day. Parents should encourage

their children to recognize their strengths and feel good about themselves. Children need to know that their parent's love is unconditional, even if acceptance of their behavior is not.

- Work with teachers, counselors, and others in the community to maximize opportunities for the child to interact with those who can provide education, guidance, and mentoring.
- Provide enjoyable activities in which the child excels—in computers, art, sports, the performing arts, etc.—in order to boost self-esteem and resiliency.
- Talk to the child about what needs to improve academically and behaviorally in a non-threatening manner.
- Consider other educational alternatives, such as home schooling, outside tutoring, therapy, etc.
- Provide positive feedback to teachers and administrators who work with the child, as this will motivate them to do even more to assist them.
- Avoid ridiculing the child or the teacher, as this can cause both to be less vigilant in their efforts.
- Avoid blaming self for the child's problems, as this can lead to feelings of depression and guilt that are not helpful to anyone. If needed, the parent should talk to a trusted friend or counselor outside the situation to discuss any feelings of frustration, guilt, worry, etc. to avoid feeling overwhelmed and alone. Parents should avoid those who speak negatively about the situation.
- Avoid comparing the child to any other child, as such comparisons can make the child feel unloved and devalued and will lessen the motivation to improve.

Teachers who are working with the academic and/or behavioral issues of their students should:

- Seek help for a child as soon as a problem becomes apparent to prevent her from falling further behind academically, or, in the case of a behavioral problem, to prevent the situation from escalating.
- Schedule a meeting with the child's parents and other relevant professionals as soon as possible to discuss how to best deal with the child's issues.
- Make a list of the positive attributes and skills of the child to cultivate feelings of hope, caring, and encouragement. This will help teachers convey caring and belief in the child's ability to succeed.
- Recognize emotional burnout when working with a child. Children are good at sensing when they are aggravating someone, or are not liked, and it will have a negative impact on their ability to learn, as well as the teacher's ability to provide effective instruction and guidance. Discuss feelings of frustration with trusted colleagues in order to gain perspective, and hopefully, to avoid burnout.
- Do not let feelings about a child with academic and/or behavioral issues negatively impact your attitude and teaching style with the rest of the class.
- Document all intervention efforts to provide accurate feedback on the child's progress as well as to inform parents and other professionals about the steps taken to remedy the situation.

To be an effective teacher, it's important to be able to respond to academic failure and misbehavior in all students. If you attempt to instruct and discipline African American children based on your own cultural frame of reference, you are setting yourself up for failure. Black children resent being educated from a viewpoint that devalues their cultural heritage. They perform best when instructors incorporate aspects of the Black experience into the curriculum and discipline them with cultural sensitivity. Remember this the next time you attempt to reprimand or give up on an African American student just because she is not assimilating into the Eurocentric mainstream.

CHAPTER 4:
CULTURALLY RESPONSIVE
INSTRUCTION

"It is a peculiar sensation, this double-consciousness, this sense of always looking at one's self through the eyes of others. . . . One ever feels his twoness, — an American, a Negro; two souls, two thoughts, two unreconciled strivings; two warring ideals in one dark body, whose dogged strength alone keeps it from being torn asunder."

W. E. B. Dubois, African American author/teacher, cofounder of the NAACP (1868–1963)

I recently watched *Redemption: The Tookie Williams Story,* a movie about the life of Nobel Prize winning, Los Angeles Crypts founder Stan "Tookie" Williams. His character was played by actor Jamie Foxx, and Lynn Winfield played the role of Barbara Bencel, an author who befriends him.

After Stan is convicted for several homicides, he changes his lifestyle and organizes a monumental pact between the Crypts and their rivals, the Bloods. He gains worldwide attention when he writes a series of anti-gang books for children and ends up winning a Nobel Peace Prize. He wrestles with his own demons and wins, and despite all of his critics and enemies, he finds redemption.

At one point in the story, Stan talks about the self-hatred and self-denial that causes African American men to destroy one another. Combine these factors with the environment in which he lived and it's easy to understand what drove Stan to help start the Los Angeles Crypts.

As a youngster, Stan Williams epitomized the African American male that has been influenced by negative stereotypes and self-fulfilling prophecies. An all too common tale, Stan's story is repeated day after day in African American communities throughout the country.

In order to be a successful teacher, educators must understand the cultures of all students, including African Americans. The concept of culture affects the way students act, speak, dress, and behave. It is becoming more and more important that teachers create a classroom environment that welcomes individual differences and rejects stereotypes. Teachers must have high expectations for all students regardless of race or socioeconomic status. Low expectations can lead to a poor self-image in Black learners and permanent damage to their sense of racial identity. Since the typical curriculum represents the values, opinions, and experiences of Anglo Saxons, Black Students often feel as if they are strangers in a foreign land.

What You Don't Know Can Hurt Your Students

A teacher's cultural background may influence her perception of what is thought to be proper behavior. This is often a problem for African American students, whose language, behavior, and learning style tend to be Afrocentric while the teachers, administrators, and school structure are Eurocentric, even when a majority of the staff is Black.

As Jacqueline Irvine (1990) points out, cultural differences are often the source of disagreements between African American students and their teachers. If White teachers are unaware of the cultural differences, they may view students' behavior negatively (Irvine 1990, p. 61). Teachers bring their own culture and values with them into the classroom, and when faced with conflicts, they tend to judge students' behavior against their own set of values. Therefore, the teacher's own perceptions and behaviors can severely impede learning in the classroom.

Cultural conflicts tend to occur most when the middle-class teacher, who is frequently White and female, considers Black male behavior as disruptive or acting out. Irvine (1990) agreed that undeniably, "teachers tend to overreact to the behavior of black students, particularly black male students."

Janice Hale-Benson (1986) points out that within their neighborhoods, Black males are encouraged to be athletic, develop sexual experiences, master the streets, and fight well. In elementary school, they learn to play "the dozens," which is a verbal combat of insulting comments to see who can be the wittiest (66).

Educational researchers and teachers continually compare African American children to their White classmates, rating them lower in achievement, IQ, creativity, reading, writing, and social interactions. This deficiency approach to the education of African American students ignores the first principle of a constructivist philosophy, which is to teach from the knowledge base of the learner (Henderson, 1996).

Preparing to Teach Diverse Students

Many teachers are poorly prepared to teach ethnically diverse student populations. Despite the growing numbers of Black students and their disproportionately poor performance, some

47

teacher education programs still hesitate to include multicultural education (Gay, 2000). Other programs are trying to figure out the most appropriate way to implement it. Only a few programs are actively and eagerly delivering multicultural education. Culturally responsive teaching asserts that specific knowledge about cultural diversity is crucial to meeting the educational needs of ethnically diverse student populations.

Part of this knowledge about cultural diversity includes understanding the cultural characteristics and contributions of different ethnic groups (King, Hollins, & Hayman, 1997). Culture covers many aspects, some of which are more important for teachers to know than others because they have direct implications for teaching and learning (Gay, 2000).

Ladson-Billings (1994) suggests the use of culturally relevant instruction as a strategy for reaching African American students and improving school success. She says that the use of culture to convey knowledge, skills, and attitudes empowers students intellectually, socially, emotionally, and politically. These cultural referents are not simply means for connecting or explaining the dominant culture; they are features of the curriculum in their own right (18).

For example, if you were attempting to teach a predominately African American class about historic rivalries like the Hatfield and McCoys or the War of the Roses, you could use the recent rap conflicts between the West Coast (Tupac) and East Coast (Notorious B.I.G.) to serve as a frame of reference. Historic and modern rivalries could be juxtaposed to show their inherent destructiveness—the only difference is that they happened in different eras.

Culturally Responsive Instruction

Teaching that revolves around the student's culture not only addresses the cognitive aspects of learning, but the emotional as well. When a student's culture is respected, she is inspired to learn because the negative self-image that comes with rejection is removed. Furthermore, an appreciation of what the student already knows encourages further learning by validating the idea that students can learn.

Teachers should be well-versed in their students' cultural values, traditions, communication styles, learning styles, contributions, and relational patterns. Gay says that teachers need to know which ethnic groups practice communal living and cooperative problem solving and how these preferences affect motivation, life goals, and task performance.

The following traits are attributed to African American culture. It is imperative that I point out that all African American Students are not alike, but the following idiosyncrasies can be observed within the African American community.

Characteristics of the African American Student

- The discussion style of many African Americans is simultaneous talk instead of alternating talk.
- African American verbal communication uses colorful language.
- African American students prefer to study while music or conversation occurs in the room.
- African American values hold that there is unity among and between all things.

- African Americans have an outer-directed rather than an egocentric focus (Ford, Obiakor, & Patton, 1995).

Incorporating Culturally Responsive Strategies

One requirement for developing a knowledge base for culturally responsive teaching is learning about the history, traditions, and idiosyncrasies of specific ethnic groups. The understanding that teachers need to have about cultural diversity should go beyond minimal awareness of, respect for, and general recognition of the fact that ethnic groups do express their values in a variety of ways.

This increased knowledge of cultural habits is needed to make schooling more interesting and stimulating for ethnically diverse students. Too many teachers believe that their content areas and cultural diversity are incompatible, and that combining them is a conceptual stretch that may prevent disciplinary integrity. Gay tells us that this is simply not true.

Misconceptions about multicultural instructional strategies arise from the fact that many teachers do not know enough about the contributions that different ethnic groups have made to their subject. They may be vaguely familiar with the accomplishments of certain well-known individuals, such as African American musicians in popular culture or politicians in city, state, and national government. However, teachers are not likely to know much about the less publicly visible but highly significant contributions of ethnic groups to science, technology, medicine, math, law, and economics.

Culturally Responsive Instruction

Educational Strategies for Celebrating the Uniqueness of African American Students

It is not necessary to be an expert on the different cultures, but it is important to be sensitive to the fact that differences do exist and that such differences must be respected. The following are some culturally-sensitive strategies that teachers can use in the classroom to bring the best out of their African American students.

- Avoid segregating students by cultural groups, and don't allow them to segregate themselves.
- Intervene immediately when a student ridicules a minority student's culture or language.
- To effectively teach minority students, you must understand how their cultural influences their classroom interactions.
- Many African American students speak regional slang. These variances must be perceived as only a difference, not a deficit or deficiency.
- Children who speak other languages or dialects should be accepted with a positive attitude and aided in the mastery of Standard American English.
- Teachers should view learning difficulties experienced by African American students as a result of cultural differences rather than indicators of an intellectual deficit.
- Use the student's culture to help the student create meaning and understanding of the world.
- Be a classroom activist. Take on different roles for different cultural backgrounds, and vary your methods of instruction to ensure that you are addressing all students.

51

- Recognize that cultural backgrounds may discourage some students from active participation in the classroom. (In some ethnic groups, volunteering a response or comment is a sign of disrespect for authority.)
- Help others (teachers, administration, parents, etc.) accept your students' cultural differences.
- Learn as much about minority students as other students.
- Respond fully to the comments of all students, especially minority and female students.
- Lead a classroom discussion on stereotyping (minority and gender) and the consequences of stereotyping. Remember that many African American students respond highly to cooperative learning.

Source: *(Ford, Obiakor, & Patton, 1995)*

The responsibility for ensuring that minorities succeed cannot rest with teachers alone. Administrators must also help. Some strategies for administrators include the following:

- Review school rules and revise policies that reprimand students for cultural habits (dress, slang, etc.).

- Tailor staff development sessions to instruct teachers on how to educate African American and other minority youth.

- Incorporate heterogeneous and cooperative groupings as opposed to ability grouping and tracking.

- Incorporate a climate of equal opportunity.

Teach with Different Learning Styles in Mind

While taking Advanced Educational Psychology, I learned several theories and techniques that were designed to facilitate effective classroom management. One of the most valuable techniques I have used is the Premack Principle, also known as "Grandma's Rule" ("Eat your peas and then you can have dessert," for example).

Case in point, I had a little girl who was highly intelligent, but during lectures and class work she would daydream instead of concentrating on the task at hand.

One day, while the students were surfing the Internet to find information for a group PowerPoint presentation, I noticed that this student loved to work on computers. The next time I caught her daydreaming during a class assignment, I made a deal with her. I promised her that if she would stay on task during the week, on Fridays during homeroom I would allow her to go to the library and surf the Internet. She agreed and for the rest of the semester she stayed on task and completed her class assignments in order to receive her coveted computer time. Since she did not have a computer at home or even access to one, being able to go to the school library was a dream come true for her.

Since traditional schools were designed for White students, educating White children has been more successful than educating Black children. African Americans have been expected to function in European-styled schools that were not designed with their learning needs in mind (Hale-Benson 1986, p. 178; 1990, p. 211).

Furthermore, if the academic performance of Black children is evaluated based on White standards (because White children are considered to be the norm by "experts"), then Black children will always be considered "deficient, deviant, pathological, or precocious" since they are never the norm (Hale-Benson 1986, p. 179–80).

Don Locke (1992) tells us that persons from the dominant culture should not use their own cultural background as a reference for how African American children should behave (pp. xi–xii, 27). Locke adds that educators must realize that it is no longer okay to use just one method of teaching for all students.

Joyce King (1994) asserts, "Teachers need sufficient in-depth understanding of their students' background to select and incorporate into the education process those forms of cultural knowledge and competence that facilitate meaningful, transformative learning" (42). Not only is a person's sense of identity reinforced by understanding their culture, but the *way* they learn is embedded in their culture. Significant changes will be made only when teacher education programs require teachers to study their own cultural backgrounds as preparation for understanding the learning power behind cultural knowledge.

Teachers must travel beyond the comfort zone of their own cultures to educate themselves in the values and habits of other racial and ethnic groups.

"While it is recognized that African Americans make up a distinct racial group, the acknowledgment that this racial group has a distinct culture is still not recognized. It is presumed that African American children are exactly like white children but just need a little extra help." (Ladson-Billings 1994, p. 9)

Guidelines for Integrating Culturally Sensitive Instruction
The solution to reducing cultural incompatibility between home and school is not necessarily to have the school reproduce every cultural aspect of the home and community (Villegas, 1991).

However, teachers must adjust and introduce cultural variables in their interactions with African American students and in their classroom lessons.

- Special education must not be the only solution for African American students whose learning and behavioral patterns are mismatched with the instructional methods of traditional schools.
- The high presence of African American students in special education programs is due to the fact that traditional instructional methods tend to be unrelated to their culture and personal experiences.
- The theory that African Americans' low achievement is due to genetic deficiencies has been debated throughout history. Effective educators do not view African American differences as genetic defects but as foundations upon which to build.
- Culturally sensitive teachers recognize and build on the strengths and interests of their students. Poplin's (1988) theory of constructivism suggests that a student's framework for learning begins with what they currently know. Consequently, teachers must develop knowledge of their learners' cultures and must create meaningful experiences around what learners know rather than what they do not know.
- When teaching, use a somewhat musical, dramatic speaking style with a variety of animated gestures. Use an assortment of techniques every day such as repetition, call-and-response, variation in pace, and alliteration to fascinate your students. The more you try to incorporate their culture

and habits into your instruction, the more likely you are to be an effective educator of African American students.

- Language used in the school may differ from what is used in the home, or it may be the same language but differs in the way it is used (Villegas, 1991). For this reason, language activities presented in the classroom may produce several different interpretations based on how the student views the world. Teachers who are not sensitive to these issues may view the responses of linguistically diverse learners as "wrong" or unintelligent.
- When learners are provided several opportunities to incorporate their cultural background, interests, and cognitive styles in the learning environment, they are more likely to experience academic success.

Marcia Fear-Fenn (1993) says that the keys to learner success are content, classroom environment, and methods and strategies that determine how the content is taught. Ongoing professional development can give teachers time to reflect on their current practices and consider what changes can be made to improve what and how they teach. For content to be effective, it must include various perspectives and depict diverse role models, which reflect a variety of ethnic groups.

Instructional strategies should adjust for different learning styles by including peer teaching, small group work, demonstrations, oral presentations, role playing, incorporation of music and art, and brainstorming to tap into prior knowledge. Teachers should make every effort to eliminate stereotyping and maintain high expectations for all students.

Ideas That Work

Because African American learners thrive on interaction with their peers, teachers should use a variety of stimuli and encourage students to work cooperatively in small groups (Kirkland-Holmes and Federlein 1990, p. 4).

African American students appreciate oral communication (Hale-Benson 1986, p. 43). Their relational style prefers the arts. Black students profit from creative and lively settings that encourage higher-order thinking skills and promote open-ended divergent thinking (Kirkland-Holmes & Federlein 1990, p. 2). In addition, they excel when learning material through self-expression in visual, dramatic, and musical arts (Hale-Benson, p. 161).

To be effective with the African American population, teachers should include the creative arts in interdisciplinary units to teach literature and history (Kirkland-Holmes & Federlein, p. 3). Students should have frequent opportunities to move around, speak, read aloud, and participate in hands-on activities (Hale-Benson, p. 78).

African American students learn best when they are asked to perform a variety of tasks relevant to their everyday lives. Teachers can relate the curriculum to personal experiences and encourage students to deal with social issues from a fair or unfair viewpoint (Hale-Benson 1986, p. 42) that are connected to peace, justice, values, economic equity, and self-esteem (Kirkland-Holmes and Federlein, p. 3).

When teaching content areas such as science or math, teachers ought to approach these subjects through the contributions of Africans (Kirkland-Holmes & Federlein, p. 2). Further, they should offer lessons that provide positive information on the culture and history of African Americans, so as to build pride in their racial heritage and cultural self-esteem (Hale-Benson, p. 161; Kirkland-Holmes & Federlein, p. 3).

Jawanza Kunjufu (1997) noted that African American children tend to be motivated by the practical and not the hypothetical. African American children generally prefer playing with real babies rather than with dolls, giving directions by pointing out landmarks rather than by observing street signs, and preparing food by trial and error rather than by following a recipe. In addition, he observed that African American children tend to remember faces and not names (41).

In her book *Other People's Children,* Lisa Delpit suggests the following practical tips for addressing different learning styles:

- When teaching writing, have students listen to rap songs in order to develop a rule base for their creation. Then have students teach the teacher and their classmates the rules for writing their rap. Transfer this concept to the rules governing the composition of other genres that will be studied.
- Have students listen to a variety of oral and written language styles and discuss the impact of those styles on the message and the likely effect on different audiences. Then recreate the texts using different language styles appropriate for different audiences such as a church group, academics, rap singers, or politicians.
- Have students interview various personnel officers in actual workplaces about their attitudes toward different styles in oral and written language. Follow up with a discussion of the interview results.
- Have students study and analyze book language. Then have the students translate the book language into a familiar language style that they are used to.

58

- Have students or groups of students create a bi-dialectal dictionary of their own language form and Standard English.
- Take a bulletin board and divide it in half. On the left side, display words or phrases from the students' writing. Label this side "Our Heritage Language." On the right side, list translations of the students' writing into Standard English. Label this list "Formal English."

Interacting with African American Students

Having an open mind as well as understanding and believing that different learning styles exist will allow educators to implement more diverse teaching styles in their classrooms, which will ultimately help students from all backgrounds.

Be Sensitive to Dialect

Teachers may occasionally insert some Black English dialect into their discussions with African American students. Only teachers who have developed a positive relationship with learners should use this type of communication; otherwise this form of interaction could be seen as demeaning. Furthermore, teachers should tell African American students that although Black English dialect is acceptable in their homes and neighborhood, it is not accepted in all situations. Even so, when the teacher uses the learner's dialect occasionally, the learner may be more willing to take on tasks he or she might otherwise refuse to do (Villegas, 1991).

Teachers should not only try to speak to Black students in a familiar way, they should also know how students interact and respond during class discussions. After numerous classroom observations, Foster noted that African American students had a tendency to blurt out comments without raising their hands more often than White students. As a result, they were viewed as troublemakers. Regardless of the fact that the students wanted to enthusiastically participate and did not need to be pushed for comments, teachers considered the active participation to be a rule violation rather than an indication of student interest (Foster, 1992).

Center Learning Around People

As stated earlier, African American students may benefit from small-group work and peer tutoring (Hale-Benson, 1986). Also, teachers should select reading materials that include realistic young people with whom African American students can relate. Select books that accentuate the learner's lifestyle, morals, desires, speech, and mannerisms (Villegas, 1991). Teachers should also select instructional materials that include a variety of ethnic groups, not just African Americans (Franklin & Mickel).

Allow Students to Work Together

When organizing instructional activities for small group work, realize that the room may not always be quiet, and some students may even stray off task at times. Nonetheless, students need to have opportunities to work on problems together and to discuss different ways of solving a problem. In addition, this approach gives students a chance to hear other opinions and to realize that there may be many methods for completing a task. Group activities also promote social development and cross-racial friendships. Small group work can include:

- Cooperative Learning: This technique involves having students work together in groups.
- Peer Tutoring: This person-to-person interaction encourages nurturing relationships between learners (Hale-Benson, 1986). With this strategy, the teacher persuades students to tutor each other and problem-solve together as part of a small group.

Change Your Attitude Toward Learning

Teachers must believe that all African American students can learn regardless of a child's behavior, language, hairstyle, or clothing, and they must make an effort to understand and accept certain culturally related behaviors.

Features of Effective Teachers

Teacher attitudes and perceptions of students can affect the academic achievement of African American learners both positively and negatively. According to Villegas (1991), an effective teacher is one who has the knack for creating meaningful and successful classroom activities that take into account the student's culture and previous experiences.

In another study, Dillon (1989) found that effective teachers were successful in connecting home and school cultures. These teachers were able to create learning environments that were open and risk free; plus they planned and implemented activities that met the interests and needs of all students.

Effective teachers link African American students' home and school cultures by using a variety of stimuli, greater verve, and verbal interaction. In order for teachers to reach African American children, they must first understand the cultural complexities of Black culture. Learning occurs when teachers step out of their comfort zone, place the learner's needs above their own desire for simplicity, and teach according to each child's individual learning style. When the instructor's teaching style and the child's learning style are in sync, meaningful dialogue and learning take place.

Teachers must focus on how best to accommodate African American learning styles and avoid evaluating Black children against a White standard. Differences in learning should be considered as such and not as differences in capability.

CHAPTER 5:
UPHOLD HIGH EXPECTATIONS

"If a man is called to be a street sweeper, he should sweep streets even as Michelangelo painted, or Beethoven composed music, or Shakespeare composed poetry. He should sweep streets so well that all the hosts of heaven and earth will pause to say, "Here lived a great street sweeper who did his job well." Martin Luther King, Jr., African American civil rights leader (1929–1967)

As imperfect human beings, it's natural for us to make judgments. A child's socioeconomic status, language ability, past performance, appearance, weight, and numerous other factors can influence our opinions of that child. What many people don't realize, however, is that the early assumptions we make often become self-fulfilling prophecies. A student labeled as gifted may succeed, while a student labeled as a troublemaker might fall behind (Gazin, 2004).

Pygmalion Effect
American children, like all children, are vulnerable to teacher expectations. The Rosenthal and Jacobson study of 1968 was the first full-length study to suggest that teacher expectations, even when based on erroneous information, can influence the academic performance of children. This harmful practice is commonly known as the Pygmalion Effect. It is also the reason

why most African American children are lost in the primary grades. The educational difficulties that they experience later on in life can be correlated with a lack of motivation or encouragement from teachers while they were in elementary school. If no interventions are implemented early on, this will manifest itself into learned helplessness later on in life (Rosenthal & Jacobson, 1968).

Also damaging are the comments often heard in the teacher's lounge such as, "That Maurice never does his homework" or "Malcolm is always causing problems." Instead of permitting negative first impressions to become permanent opinions, teachers can attempt to build a classroom environment in which every child is valued, challenged, and expected to succeed (Gazin, 2004).

In my early years, I remember the teachers who encouraged me to live up to my academic potential, but I also remember others who only paid attention to those children they deemed worthy of their attention—the light skinned, good-looking children with "good" hair, and the children of professionals and middle-class Black people. It was as if the rest of us were destined to work at the neighborhood fast food restaurant or at a local factory, so we weren't worth the time and effort. However, I knew that it wasn't something that they always did consciously, but was a manifestation of years of conditioning and exposure to racial stereotypes.

Teachers must realize that even the child with poor manners and aggressive tendencies has potential. Even though they might get on your nerves from time to time, never forget that you have been charged with a duty to educate every child, a task no different from a man who has been called to preach God's word. You don't choose the profession; the profession ultimately chooses you. You must take a vow to change the world without letting the world change you.

Uphold High Expectations

When African American students interact with teachers or other authority figures, their views of themselves are important. As Powell-Hobson and Hobson points out,

"A teacher's perception of a student leads directly to an expectation of the student. If the teacher perceives the child as intelligent, then he or she will expect above-average work from the child. A child's performance tends to mirror the expectations of his or her teachers." (Powell-Hobson & Hobson, 1992, as cited in Obiakor, 1999)

A study by Ronald Ferguson found that teachers at predominantly African American schools tend to score lower on standardized tests than teachers at mainly White schools (Ferguson, 1998). For these reasons, some argue that African American students have had a different, and inferior, educational experience compared to Whites. In other words, many believe that the U.S. public education system has not taught academic skills to African American students as effectively as it has taught them to White students (Phillips, Crouse, & Ralph, 1998).

Rosenthal and Jacobson (1968) originally proposed that teacher expectations act as self-fulfilling prophecies because student achievement reflects the expectations. Once teachers form expectations, they convey them to students through smiles, eye contact, and supportive and friendly actions. Low teacher expectations have been identified as a major obstacle to effective instruction for disenfranchised learners (Knapp, Turnbull, & Shields, 1995).

It is difficult to put aside our biases with respect to the abilities of disadvantaged students, but it is a critical first step toward effectively educating disenfranchised youth. Teachers must enter the instructional arena with a belief that all students can and will learn. Lowering academic standards and giving students easy, watered-down assignments sets the stage for reduced student achievement (Taylor & Reeves, 1993). According to Schunk (1996), teachers should not accept excuses for poor performance, nor should they develop expectations based on ethnicity or family income or any other factor unrelated to student performance.

Although many stereotypes portray African Americans as poor, in reality that is not necessarily the case. In fact, Christine Bennett (1995) pointed out that the majority of African Americans are actually middle class. Furthermore, they are employed, able to support their families as well as their churches, and able to educate their children. Despite their actual economic status, African Americans are still forced to deal with racism in the classroom, which contributes to low academic performance.

The Sadkers' (1994) research also confirms the ongoing "miseducation of black boys." As a result, Black boys tend to get lower report card grades, represent the majority of students in special education classes, and consist of the majority of school suspensions. In New York City, for example, approximately three out of four Black males never graduate, and in Milwaukee, 94 percent of all expelled students are African American boys (222).

According to Joyce King (1994), African American students caught in the middle of this cultural inequity frequently feel alienated from the school setting (40). They must also deal with pressure to reject school because doing well in school is viewed as "acting white" (Horgan 1995, p. 39).

With appropriate attitudes and respect for differences, White teachers can be effective teachers for Black students, but research shows that the presence of African American teachers in the classroom can make an even more positive difference to African American students. Rodriguez writes, "Students and teachers who share a common cognitive style tend to perceive each other more favorably than do teachers and students whose cognitive styles are dissimilar" (Rodriguez, 1983, as cited in Graybill, 1997).

Routines and Procedures

Young people respond well when they know exactly what is expected of them at all times. Young children like sameness because it gives them a sense of security. During the first week of school, a teacher's primary focus should be on teaching rules, procedures, and routines.

The first days of school, especially when dealing with African American males, will determine how the rest of your year goes. Either your kids will respect you and behave or they will be swinging from the light fixtures each and every day. Make sure you devote at least the first three or four days to teaching routines and procedure.

Many teachers attempt to instruct their students the same way they were taught. However, kids these days are a different generation, and teachers have to be on the cutting edge of their profession and develop innovative ways of reaching their students. While it is best to always use research-based techniques, who says you can't develop your own (Wong, 2001)?

Dress and act like a teacher

The most effective and efficient teachers are warm and inviting. You must always remember to address you students by their names.

Take special care not to mispronounce their names, because it is sign of disrespect. When you mispronounce a person's name, you are essentially saying, "You don't matter." People underestimate simple statements such as saying "please" or "thank you" or gestures such as thumbs up, a smile, or a pat on the back. These phrases and positive gestures signal to the recipient that you are a warm and caring person.

Gazin (2004) cites the following five tips to help teachers heighten their expectations of students:

1. Clarify expectations throughout the year by asking each student to evaluate how well she is meeting them.
2. Give students specific and appropriate praise when they achieve a goal. For example, "Emily, I am so impressed by how you provided so many details in your paragraph."
3. Share stories from your own life in order to inspire the kids. For example, "I almost failed Algebra until..."
4. Keep in mind personal details about your students, such as their favorite books.

Motivating African American Students

Dr. Shelton Wilder, the Superintendent of Schools at Hazlehurst City School District (2003–2004) in Mississippi, encouraged his employees to give themselves a pat on the back every once in a while because without periodic encouragement, most people don't feel appreciated. This advice also applies to your students. Periodic encouragement can bring out the best in all students while a lack of encouragement can stifle a student's academic and social development.

Uphold High Expectations

The need for encouragement is innate in all of us, child or adult, man or woman, Black or White. Everyone needs to feel as if someone cares about their success enough to have their efforts acknowledged along the way. However, encouragement is most needed when we are frustrated and struggling with a situation that seems overwhelming. Parents and educators must make it a priority to provide such encouragement to their children whenever they can, particularly when children are struggling academically to provide them with the greatest chance of success in school and in life.

Parents as Motivators

Parent involvement is the best predictor of a student's educational achievement because that involvement demonstrates to the student the importance of school. It also results in improved student attitudes, morale, and academic achievement. A parent's active interest leads to increased attendance, lower dropout rates, fewer discipline problems, and higher aspirations in life. Older children who have been supported this way throughout their education are also more likely to consult with parents when making important choices in life.

Teachers as Motivators

Teachers play an important role in the academic success of all the children they teach. However, it is critical that they play an even more dominant role in helping African American children who are facing academic failure and/or performing below their academic potential. Admittedly, this isn't an easy task with a classroom full of other students who also need the teacher's help and guidance.

An additional challenge for many teachers is learning to effectively cope with the differences in culture and socioeconomic status that may exist with their African American students. Such differences may include learning and social styles, as well as communication skills, and the gaps they can create between teacher and student can be frustrating and even overwhelming.

However, with proper support from colleagues and administrators, teachers can significantly improve their chances of getting through to their African American students, and in turn, increase their chance for academic success. Teachers can help students achieve this goal by:

- Having high expectations of African American students regardless of their previous academic performance.
- Helping African American students feel like a part of the school and educational community. According to Goodenow and Grady (1993), increasing a sense of school belonging (i.e., perceptions of being liked, accepted, included, respected, and encouraged to participate in school and classroom activities) may reduce the school dropout rate among African American students and other students as well.
- Creating learning environments, such as those suggested by Bandura (1993), that reinforce the view that students can master academic subjects. Students are motivated to compete with self to meet higher and higher self-determined goals. The result of such learning environments, according to Bandura, is an increased sense of self-efficacy that promotes academic achievement.

- Seeking out, discovering, and praising any effort African American students make toward learning, particularly those who are failing or underachieving. Teachers can praise any part of the learning process, academic and/or behavioral, as well as encourage the child to give self-praise. That means correcting even wrong answers in a sensitive manner. This can be done through carefully praising the effort, as opposed to diminishing the answer given.

- Assessing the learning styles of their students, keeping in mind that being different is not inferior. This information can be used to gradually incorporate learning and processing strategies that will help the child develop the skills needed to succeed in school, college, or the job market.

- Encouraging African American students to ask questions when they don't understand something or need further clarification. Many students fear appearing "stupid" in front of their classmates and/or the teacher.

- Helping students understand that taking notes and studying course material is the way to achieve academic success. Teachers can also help students develop successful test-taking strategies, an area where bright students of all races can have difficulty—to the detriment of their grades and self-esteem. Effective test preparation, relaxation techniques, and positive self-talk can be helpful in this area.

Administrators as Motivators

Even with all that teachers do in the classroom to help their students, most educators understand that the overall tone of any school is set by the administration, and most importantly, the principal. It is the principal's vision and leadership that set the bar for teaching standards, discipline, social activities, parental inclusion, student and teacher conduct, and racial and social sensitivity.

School administrators must provide teachers the training and assistance needed to increase their coping skills, instructional ability, and motivation to address the academic needs of their African American students.

Tucker (1999) recommends that such training and support include the following:

1. Motivational discussions that address the fact that when African American students fail, all students are negatively impacted.
2. Presentations by European American, African American, and Latino American teachers, as well as teachers from other ethnic groups, who have successfully improved the academic achievement of African American students who were underachieving, failing, or being disruptive in their class-rooms.
3. Presentations by African American parents that address the support, patience, and encouragement their children need and have actually received from teachers.
4. Presentations by African American students who are no longer underachieving because of the efforts of their teachers and who want to thank these teachers and share the strategies that were used to facilitate their academic success.
5. Stress management and problem solving training specifically tailored for teachers.

6. Sharing among teachers about strategies for coping with stress, frustration, and feelings of incompetence that often occur when teaching students who are underachieving and/ or academically failing.

7. Sharing among teachers about strategies that have been effective with African American students who may have inadequate academic backgrounds, skills, or motivation for certain subjects.

Research continually shows that teacher expectations of students is crucial to their performance. Jawanza Kunjufu also asserts that the most important factor in student performance is teacher and parent expectations (1997).

Obviously, the task of guiding African American children, all children, toward academic success is a complex one that requires the dedication, patience, expertise, time, hard work, and, most importantly, caring of many people. This journey toward the fulfillment of promise and potential in the children we love so well is a journey that begins in the home and branches out to schools, churches, and leaders in our communities.

If you think African American students can't learn, then they probably won't. But if you tell them they can do it and keep challenging them by offering different kinds of learning opportunities, then they will surprise you and be very successful (Wong, 1998).

Encouragement goes a long way with impressionable African American youth. On a day-to-day basis they are bombarded with images of the stereotypical Black teenager. They see themselves portrayed as unintelligent drug dealing buffoons with few redeemable qualities. When teachers, administrators, and parents encourage them to transcend their conditioning and let their actions speak louder than their words, many of these students will do almost anything to live up to our high expectations.

CHAPTER 6:
PARENT INVOLVEMENT

"It takes a whole village to raise a child." African Proverb

Parent involvement is actually the best predictor of a student's educational achievement. Parent involvement demonstrates to the student the importance of school, resulting in improved student attitudes, morals, and academic achievement. Parents' active interest also results in increased attendance, lower dropout rates, fewer discipline problems, and higher aspirations in life. Children who have been supported this way throughout their education are also more likely to consult with parents when making educational decisions.

Why, then, are some parents not involved in their student's education? First, there are varying ideas of what counts as involvement. Some believe parent involvement should focus on at-home measures to encourage learning and demonstrate the importance of education. Others believe the primary concern should be that of at-school activities that strengthen the relationship between parents and teachers.

There are several things that can hinder parental involvement. Many parents cannot visit school during the school day because they work; some parents work multiple jobs, further restricting their time at school. Also, parent involvement declines as children get older because parents often incorrectly suppose that older children need less parent involvement in their education.

Teachers and administrators are not blameless either. Some schools do not have a welcoming culture, meaning they do not actively work to involve parents in the education of their children. Others see themselves as more knowledgeable than the parents, treating the parents as their intellectual inferiors rather than equals. Some even view parents as the enemy rather than their allies and partners.

Schools that believe parents should focus on at-home behaviors are less likely to encourage parent participation in at-school activities. They may try to dissuade parents from involvement in school policy-making or academic planning. The opposite is also true. In all of these cases, it is important that parents take the initiative to become involved.

There are three fundamental keys to helping your child succeed academically. The first key is to instill in them a love of learning. The second key is to support them throughout their educational lives. The third key is to effectively communicate with your kid's school. This chapter will describe these important fundamentals and explain how to implement them in your own home. These suggestions are applicable to students of all ages and races. Simply adapt them to your child's present level of functioning.

Education is the key to our children's future, whether they attend college, take up a trade, or join the work force upon graduating from high school. There is no way to overestimate the importance of instilling the love of learning into your child because it can lead to the development of a genuine love of knowledge, not just the obligation to make good grades. When this occurs you won't have to tell your child to study because it's already his number one priority.

Parent Involvement

Are You Serious?

The other day a friend of mine was telling me a story about a mother who did not know that her child had been retained in the ninth grade. Apparently everyone in the educational system had failed this child. The teacher had attempted to schedule a conference with the child's mother, but after a couple of tries gave up. The mother worked the graveyard shift at a local factory and slept during the day.

One day she decided to visit the school and found out that her son was still in the ninth grade. Apparently the child had been doctoring his report cards and was smart enough to give himself grades similar to the ones he had gotten his whole life. The mother only glanced at his report cards to see that he was performing at an average level as usual. The lack of communication between mother and school allowed him to fall through the cracks. Once she found out about her son's failure, the mother rededicated herself to her child's education, and her son never failed again. The young man is currently in college and doing fine. There is always hope.

Instilling in Your Child a Love of Learning

Show interest! To help a child have academic success, parents must show an active interest in their child's education. This is, in fact, one of the easiest things for parents to do, and it doesn't depend on their level of education. All you have to do is set aside time every day to talk to your child about school, and don't take no for an answer.

Find the time of day your child is most willing to talk about school. If you are a working parent who is not at home when your child returns from school, make sure that you talk to as soon as you get home, or at least the first chance you get. Making sure that you periodically talk to your children demonstrates your genuine interest in their lives. Also, the lines of communication are kept open and strengthened.

Ask questions. What was the best part of your day? What was the worst? What was your best subject today? What was your worst? What was the hardest? Easiest? What did you do today that you are most proud of? What could you have done better? What project did you do in math? Who did you discuss in History today? What do you like or hate most about school? Do you like you teacher? Why not?

Ask questions about every aspect of school, but be sure to keep the conversation from becoming an interrogation. Show children that you trust them and that you are always in their corner. Your questions should be a jump-off point for a two-way conversation. Try to focus on open-ended questions that require more than yes or no answers.

An important element of showing interest is to examine your child's schoolwork and homework. You should always stay abreast of what topics your child is studying and the activities teachers are assigning. Since report cards are mailed home only a few times a year, this is an excellent way to keep up with your child's studies and grades.

Be a positive role model. Learning is a life-long discipline. Show your child your love of learning by picking up a new hobby, keeping up with current events, or reading a book. These actions will show your child that not only is one never too old to learn, but that learning should continue throughout life.

Show your child that what he is learning is an important part of being an adult. Let him see you reading in preparation for playing a fun new game with him. Use math to double a cookie recipe. Help your child understand how you use these skills at work. If you are the only parent involved in your child's life, your local Big Brothers, Big Sisters chapter can provide your child with a mentor. Through a mentoring relationship, adult volunteers and participating youth make a large commitment of their time and energy to developing relationships devoted to personal, academic, or career development and social, athletic, or artistic growth of your child (Becker, 1994).

Have reading materials available. A child's success in reading comprehension is directly related to availability of reading materials at home. Filling your home with culturally relevant books, whether your own or from the public or school library, will develop a child's comfort with books. He or she will learn that books can serve as entertainment as well as sources of knowledge.

Visit the public library often. In addition to loaning books, many libraries have children's programs for every age, from toddlers and teenagers. They also usually have a section devoted to African American Literature. Make visiting the library a family tradition.

Build on school learning. Many children think that once they leave school, learning is over. Demonstrate to your child that learning does not just occur at school. One way to do that is to plan family activities that support what your child is currently learning. If your child is studying different animals or their classifications, visit the zoo, an aquarium, or even a farm. Take your children to local historical sites when that time period is being studied. Visit government offices to get a firsthand view of how our local, state, and federal governments operate. Teach them the importance of voting and the hardships that many African

Americans had to go through in order to secure this right. Take the opportunity to talk to them about racial profiling and police brutality.

It does not matter where you visit. What is most important is that parents support and enrich their child's educational experience. Visiting these places on the Internet is just as valuable. Every parent should learn how to operate a computer. There are many community centers and schools that offer free computer training for parents. Part of being a good parent is changing with the times.

Observe your children to find out what interests them. Some children will tell you what they find interesting by discussing it endlessly. Other children need their interests to be drawn out. This just takes a bit of investigation. What topics do they bring up? What books do they check out from the library? What is their favorite subject in school? Start with an area your child already finds interesting. If you are at a complete loss, ask a teacher or one of their friends (Stipek & Seal, 2004).

Tie learning to the real world. Teachers do not always impress upon students the reason why they are learning a specific subject matter. Students often feel as though they are just learning because the teacher told them to do so. The solution is to connect learning to the real world. To do that you must first find out what your child is learning, then connect it to the everyday (Stipek & Seal, 2001).

Educational opportunities are everywhere. While grocery shopping, have your child practice math skills, whether it be counting bananas or calculating sales tax. Have your child map out the best route to the city. Learn about the birds that arrive in your backyard each spring. The following are some natural connections and examples:

- History/Social Studies and Current Events. Discuss the past and recent history of African Americans. When studying the writing of the Constitution, discuss a bill currently being argued before Congress. Teach your children that Christopher Columbus was not first person to sail to the "New World" and that an African gentleman holds that distinction (Stipek & Seal, 2001).
- Literature and Society. Read Richard Wright's *Black Boy.*
- Science and Nature. If your child is studying the stars, observe them at night. Go on a walk and chart the different types of trees you see. When studying physics, test how far differently shaped and weighted objects will travel. When studying the solar system, observe a sunset and discuss where the sun is going (Stipek & Seal, 2001).
- Math and Everyday Life. Examine how math is used in sports statistics or in measuring the distance to and from your child's favorite restaurant.

It is important that you make these connections meaningful. Find out what interests your child and tie his learning to that interest. Practice your child's new skills throughout everyday routines. Play word games and math games. Teach your child to look up information on the Internet and at the library, just so long as the topic is interesting. Discuss what you and your child observe as you each go about your day, apart and together (U. S. Department of Education, 2002).

Instilling in your child a love for learning is truly simple to do. A parent must first demonstrate his or her own love for learning.

A parent can then spark a child's interest in a topic and continue to fan that spark by showing interest.

The Right Foundation

Before focusing specifically on what a child is learning, parents must lay the foundation. This starts with a healthy lifestyle. For example, a healthy, nutritious breakfast will start the day off right and has been proven to positively affect academic achievement.

Make sure your child gets enough rest and relaxation. This means going to bed at a reasonable hour. Tired students are poor learners. Do not allow your child to stay up and watch TV because you are too weak to put your foot down.

Organization and ritual are important cornerstones of the foundation. Organization will allow for a calm and smooth morning before school, setting the appropriate tone for the day. To do this, children should wake up at a specific time, dress and prepare for school at a specific time, etc. It also helps to have the child's belongings waiting in a specific spot, preferably near the door. In fact, have her prepare her belongings the night before. This organization and ritual will make for a more pleasant morning, one in which you can express your pride in your child and allow him to calmly head out for a school day. To help keep the school week organized, you can keep a central calendar with upcoming school events, including sporting events, meetings, and report card mailings.

African American parents should set rules and consequences for their children, because they instill a sense of law

What?!

and order. These rules and consequences should be in writing but not set in stone, because there will be exceptions.

Here are some examples of home rules and consequences:

HOME RULES	CONSEQUENCES (as related to severity of the violation)
1. Curfew (for older students) • 9:00 p.m. – school nights • 10:00 p.m. – school nights: you may decide to extend their curfew for a special event • 12:00 a.m. – weekend or holiday evenings • Instruct your kids to call you if they will be late	• First offense – 45 minute earlier curfew • Second offense – grounded for at least two weeks • Third offense – grounded for up to one month; loss of certain privileges
2. School • Regularly attend all classes • Follow all school rules • No school absences without permission • Maintain at least a C+ grade average; no D's or F's • Participation in some extra-curricular activities if grades are up to par • Follow homework requirements as established by teachers; complete all assignments	• Loss of car or driving privileges for one semester • Curfew 8:00 p.m. school nights, 11:00 p.m. other nights • No outside activities until improvement is seen
3. Chores • Completes all assigned chores	• First refusal – loss of outside activity privileges for one week • Second refusal – loss of additional privileges such as car or allowance for an undisclosed amount of time

4. Dating/friends • Make sure your kids receive your permission • Tell you were they are going • Give you phone number where they will be	• First refusal – loss of outside activity privileges for one week • Second refusal – loss of additional privileges, such as car or allowance, for an undisclosed amount of time
5. Family Relationships • No disrespectful behavior or aggressive behavior toward family members	• Loss of any and all privileges
6. Drugs/Alcohol • Instruct your child to stay away from drugs and alcohol	• Various losses of privileges as deemed by the situation

Priorities

Education must be made the priority and therefore a true commitment. Be mindful of activities, whether educational or otherwise, that detract from that commitment. A child's school attendance also demonstrates the priority given to education. Your child should understand that he will attend school unless he is ill. This includes not taking him out of school for non-medical reasons.

To stress the priority of education, keep a positive attitude toward school and education in general. If you have specific concerns regarding the school or a teacher, those concerns should be addressed to the school, not your child. Your child will pick up a negative attitude and take it to school with him.

Goals and Standards

Once education is made a priority, goals and standards must be set. Standards must be high but realistic. A child should

84

understand that he should always do his best. Let him know that cheating of any type is unacceptable. Emphasize the importance of completing assignments. Other standards of education may be imposed depending on the child's age and circumstances.

Behavioral standards are also relevant to a child's educational success. These behavioral expectations, determined by each individual family, must be clearly understood. The consequences for failing to meet those standards should be clear. Children must learn that poor choices result in unpleasant consequences.

Goals differ from standards in their specificity and immediacy. While standards are more general and long-term, goals should be short-term, specific, and measurable. An appropriate goal for any age would be to earn an A on the next math test. Improving one's grade by the next report card or progress report is also an appropriate goal. Children should be expected to set their own goals, with your help. Putting goals and standards in writing and placing them in a conspicuous place may also help your child remember what he is working toward.

Encouragement and Praise

Praise is important to people of all ages, children especially. Encouragement from the most important people in their lives, their families, is priceless. Be your child's cheerleader. Let her know how proud you are of her.

This does not mean parents should ignore areas needing improvement. Encouragement includes constructive criticism when necessary. For example, instead of criticizing your child for a messy paper, suggest that his ideas will be clearer if the paper is neater.

Rewards

Almost everyone can be motivated by incentives. Incentives can range from simple stickers for younger children to special trips to the movies or the music store for older children. Rewards can also simply be praise or special time spent together. Be sure that the incentive does not overshadow the goal itself. Children should work for good grades or positive learning experiences in their own right.

Report Cards

While we know that reports cards are limited in their ability to measure intangibles such as work habits and intelligence, you should always take your child's report card seriously. Remember to praise and reward a good report card. In the event that your child does poorly or does not live up to his potential, make sure that you talk about the situation and develop an improvement plan with the teacher.

How to Effectively Communicate with Your Child's School

During my three years at Hazlehurst Middle School, I facilitated countless parent-teacher conferences and served on many Individual Education Plan (IEP) committees. Because a child's education is extremely important, all parties involved in these emotional meetings have very strong opinions. I have seen parents become confrontational in parent-teacher conferences, believing their child has been mistreated. Other parents criticize administrators, including the superintendent and principal. If, however, parents felt confident about participating in the school setting, the tension in these difficult emotional meetings could be diffused.

Most African American parents find it difficult to balance work, a family, and their child's schooling. In their book *Should I Go to the Teacher?* Susan Benjamin and Susan Sanchez talk about the benefits of effectively communicating with your child's teacher. They offer tips that will help parents avoid common misunderstandings and strengthen school-parent relationships. If you are part of a growing segment of African American parents who feel uncomfortable visiting their child's schools, remember that your tax dollars are used to pay for your child's education; you might as well check up on your investment.

If you didn't have pleasant experiences when you were in school, having to visit a school environment may feel uncomfortable. When you initially meet your child's teacher, you should approach the conference with a clear mind, seeking first to understand and then to be understood. Your child's teacher should be viewed as a valuable ally who, like you, wants to see your child succeed.

Although voicing concerns to you child's teacher may not be an easy task, it can strengthen the parent-teacher relationship and make future decisions or situations easier for you to understand and solve. When it comes to your children, it is almost impossible to remain objective because of your emotional attachment. If you feel that there is a problem that needs to be addressed, you must choose whether or not it is a good idea to confront your child's teacher. Before deciding, you should try to resolve the issue by first speaking to your child, making sure that you have all of the facts. Your child may be able to resolve the issue with his teacher alone, using you as a last resort.

A good teacher will encourage parent involvement and will go to great lengths to foster this type of partnership. When you effectively communicate with your child's school, your child's academic success will be positively affected (Benjamin & Sanchez, 1996).

Remember to empathize with a teacher's plight. They are underpaid, overworked, and underappreciated. They are expected to perform with a limited amount of resources, supplies, and assistance. True, they have holidays and summers off, but that is well deserved. Can you imagine being in a classroom everyday with 25–30 kids? Today's teachers are expected to perform more magic tricks than David Copperfield, and with the enactment of No Child Left Behind, they are under the gun to help your child succeed.

Trying to work with a parent who is convinced that the child is a perfect angel can be unbearable. If you come to a parent-teacher conference with this mindset, you are setting yourself and your child up for failure.

Parent Conferences: The First Meeting

The first time you meet your child's teacher will be of the utmost importance. You must make sure to make a good impression because it may determine how your child is treated for the remainder of the year. Showing your child's teacher that you are very concerned about his education goes a long way in today's schools.

Setting up the Conference

When setting up a parent-teacher conference with you child's teacher, make sure you agree upon a time of day when neither of you will be hurried. Treat the conference the same way you would a professional meeting or a job interview. By being prepared for your parent-teacher conference, you have already assured success. Make a list of questions for your child's teacher and bring the list with you.

The Traditional Conference

Your child spends about 180 days with his teachers. You must know how to effectively participate in the meeting in order to help your child succeed in school. The following tips will help ensure that your conference is productive:

1. Leave your personal feelings at the door, and be ready to engage in one of the most important meetings you will ever attend.
2. Speak calmly with your child's teacher. Do not criticize him or her in front of your child.
3. Listen carefully at the meeting, and don't hesitate to say what's on your mind.
4. Brace yourself for the possibility of bad news. Ask your teacher not to "sugarcoat" any of your child's negative habits.
5. Discuss the conference with your child afterwards. Give her the pros and cons of her performance, and list the corrective measures that will be taken to help her function at an optimal level.

Parent support groups like the PTA (Parent Teachers Association) provide workshops and seminars for parents. You can discover how to increase your involvement in the school as well as learn how to foster positive relationships with your child's teachers.

Student Led Conferencing

If you are lucky enough to be working with a truly progressive teacher, they may tell you that your child will be giving you a student led conference. Student led conferences have been getting rave reviews from teachers across the country. When juxtaposed against traditional parent-teacher conferences, most educators agree that student led conferences win hands down. This is how student led conferences usually work:

1. At the beginning of the school year, the teacher helps students create a binder that will serve as their portfolio. This portfolio contains the students' class assignments, homework, quizzes, tests, etc.
2. A week prior to the conference, a letter is sent home to parents informing them that their child will lead a student-teacher conference.
3. About three days before the conference, the teacher helps the student prepare a portfolio of her work, including a project, quizzes, and favorite assignment.
4. The day prior to the conference, the student rehearses his presentation and makes any necessary changes.
5. On the day of the conference, the student tells his teacher and parent(s) how he feels about his performance in school. His successes, failures, and plan for improvement are discussed.

One drawback to the student led conference is that if the parent doesn't show up, the child feels a great deal of disappointment. You can imagine the pain a child would feel if, after spending all week preparing for the conference, the parent(s) doesn't even show up.

CHAPTER 7:
HOMEWORK FOR PARENTS

"Education is our passport to the future, for tomorrow belongs to the people who prepare for it today." Malcolm X, Civil Rights Leader (1925–1965)

Children are not the only ones responsible for homework—so are parents. Your homework is to assist your child throughout her school career, so be available. The first step is to help create appropriate study habits, including a suitable atmosphere for studying. And don't say you don't have the time or the expertise to help your child with homework; many of our parents and parents' parents barely finished high school, but they still made the effort to help with homework. If it wasn't for the encouragement my father and mother gave me, I don't know where I would be right now. Although they didn't understand how to complete advanced algebraic problems, they made a valiant effort and encouraged me to be diligent with my schoolwork. That is what parent involvement is all about.

Appropriate Atmosphere
Create a specific area for studying, such as the child's bedroom or the kitchen or dining room table. It doesn't need to be fancy, just quiet and well lit. Allow your child to decorate the area to make it a more comfortable, inviting space. The study area should have enough space to hold all necessary school supplies, plus have room for your child to work (U.S. Department of Education, 2002).

If you have a small home or a noisy household, try to organize the family schedule so that the study period is a quiet one. This may mean moving other family members to a different room while your child is studying. If this is not possible, buy your child a pair of earplugs to drown out most of the noise. Providing a quiet, stable area for studying creates an environment that is conducive to learning.

Bulletin Board

A bulletin board is a simple, inexpensive way to have important school information, such as the school calendar, easily accessible. Post study tips, long-term projects, and even your child's home and school schedule on the board. Let your child add to it by decorating it with things that are important to her. If you don't have the money or space for a bulletin board, remember that posting notes on the refrigerator will do just fine.

Distractions

Keep distractions to a minimum. This means turning off the television, radio, and video games while your child is studying. Children cannot focus on their task when distracted by the television, video games, or the radio, even if it is in another room.

Television can serve as a learning tool if your child is watching educational programs, such as children's literature, science, and nature programs. However, the study hour is not the appropriate time. Although there is some value to children watching television, allowing them to spend countless hours watching Sponge Bob or playing video games is counterproductive to their intellectual growth. When possible, only purchase video and computer programs with educational content (U.S. Department of Education, 2002).

The telephone can also serve as a distraction. Limit telephone use during your child's study period to only calls needed to verify assignments or obtain additional information. Verify that these conversations are school-related. Limit telephone usage by other family members during this time so that the phone will be available if needed by your child. This is a great way to emphasize that education is the first priority.

The Internet, much like the telephone, can serve as a study aid or a distraction. As with the phone, limit Internet use by other family members during study periods, so that it is free if needed by your child for school-related work. Monitor Internet usage to verify that its use truly is informational. You can do this by blocking your child's access to websites with mature content and checking the website history of your computer daily.

School Supplies

Check with your child to determine what supplies he needs. Often schools will send home a list of needed supplies. With older children, make it their responsibility to keep track of needed supplies.

Common provisions include pens, pencils, paper, ruler, notebook, colored pencils, and erasers. Other useful supplies are a good dictionary and thesaurus, stapler and staples, scissors, maps, pencil sharpener, paper clips, tape, glue, and a calculator. If you cannot provide those, speak with the school about possible sources of help. Do not be afraid to ask for help. There are many nonprofit organizations that hand out free school supplies to needy families (U.S. Department of Education, 2002).

Computers are a great educational resource, useful for everything from typing papers and reports to Internet research. However, homework can still be successfully completed even if you do not have one at home. School libraries and public libraries often provide time for school-related computer usage, including Internet research. Today, computers are becoming increasingly affordable. You can get a brand new desktop for under $800 that comes with six months of free time on AOL (America Online), word processing programs, and more from most manufacturers (U.S. Department of Education, 2002).

Provide a book bag or backpack for your child to carry schoolwork and books between school and home. This will help keep your child organized and help you to monitor his schoolwork. Keep your child's assignment notebook in the bag, too. This is a great way to help him stay organized.

Make sure your child knows the importance of keeping up with his textbooks. I have seen parents spend up to $120 to replace textbooks that their child either lost or damaged. Remember, your parents didn't let you get away with this sort of behavior, so why should you let yours?

A Regular Time for Homework

A specific time to complete homework should be set aside everyday, preferably at the same time every day. The hour is unimportant. The key is that homework is done at a regular time every day. The best schedule is the one that works for your family's unique situation and is adaptable, depending on the age of your child and her individual needs. Some children study best immediately after school. Others can focus better after dinner. Still others need dinner as a study break. Experiment to see what time works best for your child and your family. This study time may need to be flexible, depending on extracurricular activities (U.S. Department of Education, 2002).

Requiring your child to spend a specific amount of time studying or participating in some other learning activity each day may also work well. Knowing that the time period must be filled with learning may help those children who tend to "forget" assignments or rush through to completion (U.S. Department of Education, 2002).

Help your child develop a written schedule specifying his regular time for homework. This should be placed in a conspicuous place, such as the study area bulletin board.

Appointment Book and Calendar

Provide your child with a small book or notepad to keep track of assignments, including requirements and due date so as to reduce confusion. Younger children will need help with this. Add information such as school activities or extracurricular activities. This will help keep your child on top of her assignments.

Parents can easily model appropriate behavior by using their appointment book to list daily chores, shopping lists, and appointments. The ability to prioritize will serve your children well in the real world.

Students should also have access to a large wall calendar. Mark important dates such as exams, project deadlines, and school activities on the calendar so that your child will have a big-picture view of the semester. Showing your child the big picture will prevent last-minute surprises and minimize procrastination. Feel free to color-code activities, with tests in one color and projects in another, for example.

Breaks

Allow for regular but short study breaks. Teenagers can focus for at least an hour before needing a study break, while younger children may only last 15 minutes, so adjust study periods accordingly. Breaks can even be viewed as rewards for finishing a subject or specific activity.

Homework

Homework is about more than just studying. Especially in the higher grades, poor grades are the result of insufficient effort as opposed to lack of knowledge.

Teachers assign homework for a variety of reasons. Homework helps students:

- Review and practice skills and concepts learned in class
- Prepare for the next day's learning
- Utilize resources, including the Internet, reference materials, and libraries, to find additional information about a subject
- Assimilate learning by applying multiple skills and concepts together in high-level thinking
- Develop good study skills
- Work independently
- Develop self-discipline and responsibility.

Source: (U.S. Department of Education, 2002)

Homework also allows teachers and parents to monitor student understanding. Moreover, monitoring homework can help keep families engaged in the schools (U.S. Department of Education, 2002).

Homework for Parents

Be sure to find out about the school's homework policy. Some school districts have school-wide homework policies, while in others the individual teacher decides. The homework policy should discuss expectations, rules, and guidelines. Find out if teachers expect parents to closely monitor school work or just check periodically to verify assignments are being completed.

The homework policy may discuss the amount of time students are expected to study every night. The appropriate amount of homework depends on the age of the child. Children in kindergarten through second grade should study 10 to 20 minutes per day. Children between the third and sixth grades should study 30 to 60 minutes per day. High school students should study at least two hours per night, although that amount will likely vary. If you are concerned about the amount of homework your child is receiving, be sure to speak to his teachers (U.S. Department of Education, 2002).

Monitor homework and studying. Parents must monitor studying and homework time to support the child's education and show that it is the first priority. How can you expect your child to make education a top priority if you don't make it yours?

Monitoring your child's homework is simple. The first step is to simply be available to answer questions or provide help when needed.

Talk about the assignment. Does the child understand what he needs to do? If not, what information does he need to understand it? Is your child missing part of the assignment? Can he call a friend? Does the school have a homework hotline or website to check for further information? With younger children, help them find the information needed to complete the assignment.

Does the child understand how to do the assignment? Is there more that he needs to learn to complete the assignment? Does he know how to apply the concept he learned in school to the assignment? Help clarify the concept if you can, however, your child must complete the assignment on his own. Does the child have the necessary supplies? Try to keep often-used supplies available for your child (U.S. Department of Education, 2002).

Check assignments for completion and general correctness. Does your child understand the work? Is she completing assignments to the best of her ability? If not, ask questions to clarify. Does she need a tutor? Is she feeling overworked? Remember to praise your child for a job well done!

Parents may also want to ask if the teacher has a system, such as voicemail or a website, for parents to check to verify homework assignments.

Should you help with the homework itself? This depends on the situation and age of the child. A general rule of thumb is to not do the work for your child. Remember, it is still the child's assignment. Let him make mistakes. Taking responsibility for one's own work and mistakes is an important part of the learning process. Additionally, most teachers gauge student understanding by their homework assignments. Doing your child's work for him will result in the teacher incorrectly assuming that your child understands the work.

Keep in mind that these suggestions should be adapted to your child's age and needs. Younger children need much more supervision. This does not mean you should not monitor teenagers, but allow them to assume more responsibility for their work. Beware of becoming too involved in your child's work, as that will prevent them from becoming independent and responsible.

An added benefit of monitoring your child's studies is that it will allow you to better understand school expectations and keep up with your child's grades. It is much easier to reverse a pattern of sliding grades when caught early.

Keep an eye out for frustration. If your child is upset, frustrated, or angry, learning cannot occur. Allow the child to take a break or try to constructively guide him in the right direction. Sometimes the best thing to do is simply to put it away and revisit it the next day.

Because studying includes more than just completing homework assignments, organization is critical to success. Encourage your child to do the following:

- Take notes. Children should take notes while reading, including summarizing the material in their own words. Note taking is an important skill, but one that is often neglected in school. There are many methods of note taking, so ask your child's teacher what form she prefers or is taught by the school.
- Should your child rewrite notes? Only if those notes will be used for reviewing. In fact, copying one's notes is a good way to review the concepts and organize them in one's mind (U.S. Department of Education, 2002).
- Study tables and charts.
- Use flashcards for quick reviews.

For questions regarding study methods, talk to your child's teacher. The school may have specific procedures for students to use.

Also, when your child is absent, he must obtain the missed work. With younger kids on an extended absence due to illness, you may need to contact the school to get the work. Teenagers should be responsible for obtaining their own work, but verify that they have done so. Because preparing a list of missing assignments for absent students is a time consuming chore for teachers that takes time from class planning, be sure your child actually completes the work.

It is a parent's responsibility to make sure a child arrives at school promptly and regularly. A child cannot be academically successful if he is not there. Poor attendance and tardiness can only harm a child's understanding of the schoolwork. Children should always be in school unless ill.

Tests

In addition to being one of the primary ways in which grades are determined, tests are increasingly being utilized for school rankings or graduation requirements. For these reasons, testing may cause some children extra stress.

To help you child do well on tests, have your child:
- Get a good night's sleep
- Carefully read testing directions
- Skip more difficult questions, and return to them later
- Relax
- Bring an extra pen or pencil (Dietel, 2004).

Parents can help by giving practice tests. For example, run math drills or read the spelling words for your child. Importantly, encourage regular studying so that he is prepared and will not have to cram for a test (U.S. Department of Education, 2002).

Extracurricular Activities

Your child's study schedule may need to be flexible, depending on extracurricular activities such as sports, dance, or music lessons, whether school-based or outside of school. If those take too much time away from study and your child does not have time to finish his or her homework, your child may need to drop an activity. Make sure homework remains a high priority. Remember, academics first, athletics second (U.S. Department of Education, 2002).

Children participate in extracurricular activities, sometimes called co-curricular activities, for a variety of reasons. They allow some children to learn new skills, develop a talent, practice sportsmanship, and experience cooperation. For others, it's just good exercise. Still others are padding their resumes for college. Whatever the reasons, most extracurricular activities provide the following multiple benefits:

- **Broadens horizons.** Extracurricular activities provide your child with additional learning experiences outside of the classroom. These learning experiences can be anything from a new sport to art and music. They often fill the gap of subjects and activities that are no longer offered by schools due to budget tightening.

- **Physical fitness.** Joining a sports team or taking up dance is an excellent way to keep your child fit and away from the TV and video games.

- **Learn social skills and team spirit.** Children learn how to become team players—an important lesson needed for success in life. Playing on a team also builds social skills as students interact with peers.

- **Time management.** Children will need to organize and manage their time better when they participate in extracurricular activities. This, too, is a valuable lesson for lifetime success.
- **Confidence building.** Some children's gifts lie in activities outside of the classroom. Extracurricular activities will allow those students to excel, building their confidence.

Students who are disengaged from school and at-risk of dropping out often benefit greatly from extracurricular activities. Joining a school athletic team will often give them a reason to remain in school. This in turn will increase self-esteem and help with peer relationships by allowing them to be part of a group (U.S. Department of Education, 2002).

On the other hand, although extracurricular activities can be beneficial, they can also add too much stress to your child's life. Be sure that your child is truly benefiting from the extra activities and is not overwhelmed by these commitments. If her grades fall, cut some of the activities. Education must remain the priority. In fact, some states and school districts have passed requirements that students cannot participate in school-based extracurricular activities unless they have passing grades (U.S. Department of Education, 2002).

Although some parents may have had a horrible experience in their own schooling, they need to put those negative feelings aside so they will not be passed on to their children. Children should view school in a positive light, regardless of what your feelings may be.

To help students succeed academically, parents should:
- Create a specific area for studying.

Homework for Parents

- Keep distractions to a minimum. That means no television, computer, video games, or phone (unless school assignments are being verified).
- Provide necessary school supplies.
- Schedule a regular time for homework to be done each day.
- Encourage short study breaks if needed.
- Monitor and check homework.
- Allow absences only when child is ill.
- Make sure extracurricular activities don't overwhelm the child and take away from learning.

CHAPTER 8:
CLOSING THE ACHIEVEMENT GAP

"If a man hasn't discovered something that he will die for, he isn't fit to live."
Martin Luther King Jr., African-American civil rights leader (1929–1967)

The achievement gap is the measured disparity in intellective competence and academic ability that separates students of color and low-income from more affluent, primarily White students. There are many gaps that include individual, institutional, and community factors. The achievement gap is defined to include measures of intellective competence as well as academic ability. Intellective competence, not to be confused with intelligence or subject matter knowledge, is a systematic method of reasoning and inferring patterns from one's environment and using them to maintain practices and invent new ones. Academic ability is an expression of intellective competence. Both academic ability and intellective competence are dynamically developable qualities. A report by the National Study Group for the Affirmative Development of Academic Ability (Bennett, et al, 2004) establishes academic ability and intellective competence as outlined in Table 1.

TABLE 1

Academic Ability Includes Capabilities in:	Intellective Competency Includes the Ability:
Literacy and numeric.	To bring order to the chaos created by information overload
Mathematical and verbal reasoning.	To reason
Skill in creating, recognizing and resolving relationships.	To uncover relationships between phenomena
Problem solving from both abstract and concrete situations, as in deductive and inductive reasoning.	To use comparison, context, intent, and values in arriving at judgments
Sensitivity to multiple contexts and perspectives.	
Skill in accessing and managing disparate bodies and chunks of information.	
Resource recognition and utilization (help seeking).	
Self-regulation.	

Developing academic abilities is necessary for students to make use of the mental processes required to solve problems and develop intellective competence. The development of academic ability, and thus intellective competence, focuses on what students should be and become as opposed to traditional measures of achievement that focus on what students know and know how to do. These developed abilities and competencies are respected and sought universally.

Closing the Achievement Gap

Intellective competence is developable through a combination of interventions in the school, home, and community. The development of intellective competence will require diverse and varied approaches to instruction that focus on the transfer of knowledge and practices. Necessary approaches to instruction and knowledge transfer have been studied and proven effective in developing the academic ability and intellective competence necessary to close the achievement gap. More importantly, these approaches are within reach.

Methods Used to Measure the Achievement Gap

Constructive measures designed to measure gaps in educational achievement have been implemented in educational systems since the 1960s. The earliest noted and documented of these early attempts is found in the research lead by James S. Coleman in response to Civil Rights Act of 1964 (Kiviat, 2001). Coleman, then a professor in the Department of Social Relations at Johns Hopkins University in Maryland, was commissioned by the U.S. Department of Education to report on the equality of educational opportunity. The Coleman Report was published in 1966. This pioneer study on educational achievement concluded that poverty was the root cause for the disparity in educational achievement. Since that time, many studies and experiments have addressed the issue of disparity, with varying conclusions. Today's initiatives are focused on multiple factors, with the understanding that multiple solutions are required.

The achievement gap is measured by several factors to include:

- Placement on standardized test scores
- Advanced placement (AP) course participation
- Advanced placement testing
- High school graduation rates
- Numbers entering college
- College graduation rates
- Earned income rates

The achievement gap is measured within the typical timelines of student education, Pre-K through college, though expert analyses suggest that gaps in achievement and intellective competence exist prior to children's entrance to Pre-K (Lee, in press).

There is no defined method to measure the achievement gap. The type and extent of testing, experimentation, data collection, and data analysis chosen for measurements are dependent upon individual goals, focus, and the population under evaluation.

How Big Is the Achievement Gap?

Scores obtained from the National Assessment of Educational Progress (NAEP) test are a commonly used measure of achievement. Federal law dictates that NAEP assessments are voluntary except in the case of states and school districts receiving Title I funding as administered by the federal government. NAEP reading and mathematics assessment tests are mandated at the fourth and eighth grades for all states and selected school districts receiving Title I funding.

Closing the Achievement Gap

The NAEP test data for the year 2003 (Department of Education, 2003), for example, reveals that African American, Hispanic, and American Indian students failed to reach the basic level of achievement at both the fourth and eighth grade levels of reading in significant numbers as compared to White and Asian students. Results from the test are summarized in Table 2.

TABLE 2

NAEP Test Results Students Reading at or Above Basic Grade Levels (2003)		
Ethnicity	4th Grade	8th Grade
African-American	40%	54%
Hispanic	44%	56%
American Indian	47%	57%
White	75%	83%
Asian	70%	79%

Another measure of the achievement gap is displayed by the disparity in numbers of students participating in AP testing. The Education Trust, Inc. promotes high academic achievement for students from kindergarten through college by working side-by-side with policy makers, parents, educational professionals, and community and business leaders around the country. The Education Trust assists in the transformation of educational institutions to serve all students and share lessons learned at the institutions with policy makers. A report by The Education Trust (Education Trust, 2003) indicates that African American and Latino students are underrepresented in AP testing, as compared to their numbers in student populations. Test results are summarized at Table 3.

TABLE 3

Student Participation in AP Test (2000–2001)			
Ethnicity	Percent of Student Population	Participants in AP Calculus Test	Participants in AP Biology Test
African-American	17%	5%	6%
Latino	17%	7%	7%
White	62%	73%	70%
Asian	4%	16%	18%

Graduation rates are also used to assess the achievement gap as indicated in the Education Trust report (Education Trust, 2003).

Closing the Achievement Gap

The report indicates that far more African American and Latino students fail to complete four-year college programs than their White and Asian counterparts. The data is summarized at Table 4.

TABLE 4

Ethnicity	College Graduates (enrolled in 1998, graduated 2002)
African-American	39%
Latino	36%
White	58%
Asian	63%

These are just a few examples of the many data sets, resulting from tests, experiments, and studies, available to measure the achievement gap.

Causes of Achievement Gaps

There are many reasons why the achievement gap exists. The issues are both diverse and complex, making solutions difficult and complex to ascertain. Some of the most commonly noted and studied causes of the achievement gap include:

- Poverty
- Race
- Lack of resources
- Teacher quality
- Student-teacher relationships

111

Approaches and Practices to Close the Achievement Gap

The ability to learn is a developmental activity that can be systematically developed with the proper tools. The following section will examine approaches to closing academic achievement gaps between students. We will also examine practices, programs, and policies that have been implemented, and assess their effectiveness in reducing the achievement gap. The section, Studies of Methods to Reduce or Eliminate the Achievement Gap, outlines these studies as they apply to the achievement gap. The section, An Active Method of Reducing the Achievement Gap, outlines the Knowledge Is Power Program (KIPP) that is effectively reducing the gap for inner city and rural African American students.

Collaborative Intervention

Schools and educational institutions are an extension of the total environment in which children learn. The home and community also play a fundamental role in developing intellective competences. Here we have one of the primary factors in the disparity. Students, primarily those of African American, Hispanic, and Native American descent, who live in economically oppressed and depressed community environments, tend to explore, interpret, and build upon much different situations than their more affluent counterparts. Efforts to close the achievement gap must take into account the socioeconomic and other cultural differences that exist outside of the school and develop a systematic approach that provides for collaborative interventions, inclusive of the school, community, and home.

Educators and the School

Knowledge that is acquired by students from their home and community environments is considered "prior knowledge" that students introduce into their school environment. Prior knowledge affects the student's ability to learn and acquire new knowledge. New knowledge will make little sense to a student when it is in conflict with what was previously constructed in the student's mind. The new knowledge, therefore, may not be properly transferred to the student and available for use in other environments. The prior knowledge may often be incomplete, inaccurate, and in conflict with the instructional demands of the school. To alleviate this conflict and eliminate confusion for the student, teachers must implement strategies to refocus the learning process to include all acquired knowledge.

Teaching for **knowledge acquisition** implies that the teacher must devote time to discovering what prior knowledge a child has acquired in order to teach the child to build on that knowledge. A question-and-answer technique should be developed so that teacher and student can learn together. Both student and teacher are then capable of gathering new information, analyzing the transferred information, and discarding incorrect or inaccurate explanations dynamically, using their collective thought processes.

Teaching for **improved comprehension** involves two concepts, consolidation and automaticity. Consolidation is the ability to explain concepts as they are retained in long-term memory. Automaticity is the ability to perform complex tasks without effort or conscious awareness. The consolidation of knowledge through learning automaticity frees the student's mental capacities for use in other activities requiring mental effort. The excess memory capacity, resulting from effective consolidation and automaticity, is necessary to initiate the information processing required for a student to comprehend. Practice is necessary to ensure that comprehension is automatic. In reading, as the practice of recognizing and deciphering words is consolidated to automaticity, memory becomes available for the information processes required in reading comprehension. The student transitions from "learning to read" to "reading to learn." The more students practice essential skills, the better the student is able to comprehend.

Learning transfers are established when the student is capable of connecting skill and knowledge *acquired* in one context with skill and knowledge *used* in another context. Teaching methods that engage the student in knowledge acquisition, improved comprehension, and deep understanding rely on effective learning transfers. The transfer of knowledge is best understood when the teacher is capable of modeling the transfer concept by providing examples of use. The student should also be shown how to apply the solution to other relevant problems. Teachers are encouraged to include visual and spatial forms of representation as alternatives to verbal and one-dimensional methods in the transference and processing of knowledge.

Teachers and schools must work together to provide **trusting environments** for students to adequately transfer knowledge. Students need assurance that they are being provided a fair environment in which to learn, and they need to feel accepted in the environment. Students feel threatened when administrators and teachers make unfair stereotypical judgments based on race and ethnicity. Anxieties about prejudice and exclusion may lessen student involvement in academic and extracurricular activities. When people of color serve as teachers, administrators, and other authority figures, the environment becomes less hostile and more inclusive.

The Community

Communities have a direct impact on the development of intellective competence in students. The community is responsible for monitoring and influencing decisions by school administrators and governing bodies to develop positive, effective learning environments for students. Community members must participate and intervene in school board decisions affecting their community and stay abreast of decisions affecting the funding of libraries, cultural institutions, and other academic support systems. Schools must partner with the community to provide students with opportunities to participate in outreach programs, such as community service.

The Home

The home should provide students with materials, models, assistance, and an environment conducive to learning. Too often, students of color are denied the things they need because of finances and the lack of access to information and resources. But these shortcomings do not have to have a negative impact on student achievement. Intellective competence, accomplished through routine activities, can still be achieved in disadvantaged home environments. Families and community organizations must become informed of and involved in both routine and high performance learning activities. Schools should recognize the home environment as a supplementary source of education and help guide the development of activities within the family's capacity. These activities should include any and all family members. Learning should be a holistic family affair.

Studies of Methods to Reduce or Eliminate the Gap

The North Central Regional Educational Laboratory (NCREL) funded a series of four studies in 2003 to examine currently implemented practices to reduce or eliminate achievement gaps. The studies examine a number of diverse approaches to closing the achievement gap in four separate and distinct scenarios: elementary school, high school, college, and rural America.

Elementary School

BASRC (Bay Area School Reform Collaborative), a 501 (c) (3) nonprofit organization, was founded in 1995 and is located in San Francisco, California. BASRC works with educators from a diverse network of schools and districts to provide schools and districts with a flexible support system that enables the educational systems to respond to changing policy mandates, funding levels, demographics, local needs, and priorities. The BASRC Achievement Gap Study compared schools in the BASRC network that were successful in narrowing the gap between African American/Latino students and White/Asian students to schools that were not. In the analysis of the 1998–1999 and 2001–2002 school years, 32 BASRC schools were equally divided into gap-closing and non-gap-closing schools based on California's Academic Performance Index (API) scores.

The study found that 16 schools experienced gap-closing growth in API scores while the non-gap-closing schools widened the gap over the four-year period. An analysis of practices and methods reveals that gap-closing schools:

- Examine strengths and weaknesses through the use of data analysis (which factor in race, socioeconomics, etc.)
- Try new strategies with the support of school leaders (collaboration)
- Evaluate the progress of students in the wake of these analyses and strategies.

Annual, standardized tests have been instrumental in developing methods to assess both student and general school performance for governing bodies and political entities. However, they have not proven effective in helping school leaders and teachers assess individual performance characteristics that are required to institute improvement processes. Teachers and school leaders require highly detailed diagnostic assessments, provided on a frequent basis, to assess students' strengths and weaknesses. For effective change to be made in schools, data must accurately represent the disparities underlying the achievement gap as they exist in classrooms. Relevant, reliable, and timely data will provide teachers and leaders with the tools they need to dynamically address measured strengths and weaknesses.

Teachers need professional development to help them understand how to analyze and apply data to methods of effective instruction for low-achieving students. Professional development should be available to teachers on a weekly, or at least, a monthly basis and should include information on how to understand, manipulate, and interpret data.

Data must include total classroom and/or school performance, and it must be interpreted and manipulated on a scheduled basis to reveal a complete portrait of strengths and weaknesses. School leaders must encourage, inquire about, and be responsive to data collection, analysis, and applied methodologies that are designed to reduce and eliminate the gap.

School leaders must provide time for the professional development of its educators. Professional development should be incorporated into the scope of the normal work week.

School leaders must set measurable goals for professional development programs. Teachers must have time to collaborate and share instructional strategies that address the issues, both general and specific. They should have time, on a regular basis, to collaborate and discuss performance data, examine results, and develop next-step strategies for low-achieving students.

Time should be scheduled for teachers to visit each other's classrooms to examine and evaluate instructional strategies on a monthly basis. This fact-finding, solution-seeking collaboration should be exercised within and across grade levels, faculty, and staff.

Teachers and school leaders need to be more open about race, addressing problems directly through discussion as well as changing and implementing policies to resolve race-based issues. As professionals, teachers and school leaders should address race issues within the context of learning and classroom instruction. Teachers and school leaders are expected to be professional when discussing the failure or advancement of students; they must not call students degrading names such as dumb or stupid.

As race is openly discussed, no longer can issues be ignored and dismissed under the pretense of color blindness. Race must be factored into the analysis of the data, and it must be respected by all persons who are committed to developing methodologies to eliminate the achievement gap.

School leaders must set measurable, equitable goals and plans for all students—for example, for all students to read above grade level. If data shows that Latino and African American students are reading below grade level, clearly some new classroom instruction needs to be implemented to address this issue. The new instruction must enhance the reading skills of the two racial groups without hindering the progressive instruction of the rest of the student population.

While data should be collected and analyzed for student performance in all subjects, reading should be given priority. The ability to read (literacy) has widespread implications and applications within and outside of the learning environment. Educators agree that assessments should be administered frequently to stay on top of student progress and difficulties. Students should read at least two and one-half hours a day. For maximum effectiveness, reading should be integrated into other subjects, including math, science, and social studies. School leaders should ensure that all teachers receive professional development in reading instruction as well as the necessary materials to target individual student needs (NCREL, 2003).

High School

The second study funded by NCREL examines the impact of The Freshman Reading Intervention literacy program developed for students at Metro High School in Chicago. The program was implemented to provide ninth grade students who scored below the 50th percentile on the reading section of the eighth grade

Explore® test additional reading instruction. The study assesses the impact of additional instruction on enhancing reading comprehension and academic performance. The literacy program also emphasizes teacher support for student achievement.

Students enrolled in the intervention program spent additional time on reading activities outside of their coursework. The program has not been proven to increase comprehension, particularly of school materials.

GPA scores increased at faster rates for students participating in the intervention program than for non-participants. Students' GPA scores rose from below 2.0 to above that level. This rise in GPA made students eligible for extracurricular activities, which was in turn expected to increase overall school commitment and self-esteem.

Students bonded with teachers who reached out, encouraged, and maintained high expectations of them. Through one-on-one interactions, teachers were better able to recognize the academic and personal needs of the student. Students were more receptive to praise and critiques from authority figures they trusted.

Overall, the intervention proved to be positive in building student-teacher relationships and improving leisure reading. Some goals were achieved and others were not. The methods developed show promise and warrant further evaluation.

Interestingly, the findings suggest that the methods could be adapted to adult learning environments. The most important finding, however, was that students should not be abruptly cut-off from the intervention and teacher relationship. Students should continue to receive support with perhaps less intense interventions and gradual exits from the process (NCREL, 2003).

Closing the Achievement Gap

College

The third study funded by NCREL examines the Meyerhoff Scholars Program at the University of Maryland-Baltimore County (UMBC), a college-level program designed to support students of color majoring in science, engineering, mathematics, and technology. Support is provided through the provision of challenges, resources, and opportunities. Since its inception in 1988, Meyerhoff has become a national leader in retaining minority students and matriculating minority graduates to postgraduate study and research careers in science and engineering.

Meyerhoff is grounded in sound theories, research, and practice. Students receive full or partial scholarships, mentors, tutors, academic advising, special Summer Bridge classes in mathematics, chemistry, and humanities, family involvement activities, and shared living space with other participants. These components supplement the academic achievements of the students and provide an environment conducive to academic and social integration as well as knowledge and skill development. The students are also provided support, motivation, monitoring, and advising.

Meyerhoff builds socially and emotionally stable environments through continuous formal and informal interactions with program staff, former program participants, and enrolled students. Prospective freshmen are introduced to the college experience, and Meyerhoff expectations are described in an orientation known as the Summer Bridge. Summer Bridge is just one of the many tools used in the program, which is designed to create a cohesive population of underrepresented students of color. This cohesive environment helps students develop the skills and confidence they'll need to interact with other diverse groups. They learn how to manage their time and stress so that they're prepared to meet expectations for behavior.

Meyerhoff provides supplemental teaching and tutoring to help students master coursework in their respective areas of study. Study groups, teaching assistants (upper classmen), and test-and-note banks have proven more effective, both psychologically and academically, than conventional approaches, such as remedial classes.

Financial capital has long been a barrier for minority students seeking higher education, creating both psychological and academic pressures that affect performance and motivation. Meyerhoff gives students access to scholarships and other financial resources.

Students receive valuable mentoring from other students and experienced professionals, making this "human capital" available for one-on-one interactions. The program provides a family-like social and academic support system made up of faculty, staff, other enrolled students, and program graduates to substitute for social networks from which minority students have traditionally been excluded.

Faculty and staff interact with students to help them make decisions about coursework selection and next-steps of study. These interactions help avert distracting academic and personal issues.

Further, freshmen have limited math, science, and engineering course loads to allow them time to adjust to college and campus life. This may mean that the students receive their degree in five years rather than four.

Meyerhoff is clearly an established and proven model for closing the achievement gap. The program components, used to supplement academic achievement, are transferable to K–12 school systems and educational services. Educators and policy makers must be willing to institute these programs and provide the resources to implement them (NCREL, 2003).

Rural America

The final study funded by NCREL, the Rural Achievement Study, is an assessment of five rural school districts in Michigan and the factors contributing to the achievement gap that exist between poor and disadvantaged students and their more advantaged counterparts. Traditionally, achievement gaps are measured in urban areas, with data generalized to rural populations.

Rural communities are defined as has having populations of less than 2,500 people. One-third of the nation's schools and 21 percent of public school students attend schools that are located within rural communities. The Rural Achievement Study describes student achievement in five rural districts and discusses processes, with respect to achievement, at both school and district levels.

The study found that smaller rural schools suffered more dramatic funding issues than larger rural schools. Poverty was the most prominent factor that negatively impacted teacher-student interactions. Issues of respect were prevalent and served to separate the general population from both school teachers and school leaders. The sometimes hostile feelings between the community and school provided distracted parents, teachers, and school leaders from the goal of educating students. Despite poverty and its

123

implications for schools and communities, race, not poverty, was the single issue studied.

District level expenditures in rural communities are, in general, based on population. While all rural schools lack resources, such as adequate facilities, course materials, educational programs, and professional development (as compared to urban schools), these resources were found to be nonexistent in some of the smaller rural communities. Larger districts are more adequately funded than smaller, isolated districts. As a result, larger districts are better able to recruit and retain qualified faculty and administrators, as well as fund professional development opportunities. School boards of the larger districts are more accountable and focused on standards and academic achievement.

Smaller rural districts, on the other hand, are dependent on grants to incorporate initiatives. They lack the funds and resources to provide equitable salaries and professional development. They are also likely to be denied on bond issues and may have school boards that are not accountable for academic achievement. These issues create a counterproductive barrier that separates the community from teachers, school, and district representatives (NCREL, 2003).

A Method of Reducing the Achievement Gap

While education experts continue to study and dialogue about the achievement gap, one group is actively working to close the gap. Teachers, administrators, and supporters of the Knowledge Is Power Program (KIPP) have implemented an unparalleled program that is effectively reducing the achievement gap for primarily African American students.

Closing the Achievement Gap

KIPP public middle school schools offer a free college-preparatory curriculum for students. These schools are open to all minorities within reach of a school and make no preference for prior academics, conduct, or income. Most students that complete KIPP's four-year curricula (fifth through eighth grade) are promoted to some of the best and most competitive college-preparatory high schools, and they go on to four-year colleges and universities. KIPP student alumni can receive additional social, academic, and financial counseling throughout their college tenure.

KIPP schools incorporate five operating principles known as the Five Pillars. They include:

1. **High expectations**. KIPP schools have defined measurable expectations for both academic performance and behavior. These expectations are supplemented by a system of rewards and consequences. Despite their socioeconomic backgrounds, the students, mostly African American, enrolled in KIPP schools are meeting and exceeding these expectations in record numbers. KIPP schools have met the goal of developing the intellective competence that educational research indicates is necessary to close the achievement gap.

2. **Choice and commitment.** Enrollment and participation in KIPP schools is by choice. Students, parents, and teachers are required to sign a contract commitment that could lead to dismissal for noncompliance. As part of the contract, teachers, parents, and students commit to timeliness, availability, doing their best, and behaviors that serve to protect the safety, rights, and interests of all in the classroom. KIPP deconstructs the stereotype that suggests that African American parents do not have the same concern for the education of their children as

other groups. Parents of KIPP students must adhere to their commitments, and the KIPP program does not accept excuses and short cuts. A student's tenure is just as dependent on the parent's choice and commitment as his or her own.

3. **More time.** The KIPP school day, school week, and school year extend beyond the schedules of traditional public schools. The school day begins at 7:30 a.m. and ends at 5:00 p.m. The school week is extended to include four hours on Saturday; the school year is extended to include one month of summer school. Teachers, parents, and students commit to the school schedule and maintain an average attendance rate of 96 percent. In addition, KIPP students complete a minimum of two hours of homework per night and are provided with their teacher's cellular phone number should they require assistance.

4. **Power to lead.** KIPP school principals are required to manage the budget and personnel. They are expected and are given permission to modify the budget and staff to maximize effectiveness. To assist principals in controlling the school environment, KIPP recruits and hires strong and effective teachers who are dedicated to motivating African American students to achieve academic success.

5. **Focus on results**. Expectations are high that students will perform at or above grade level on standardized tests and other objective measures of performance. The increased school time allows teachers to nurture students' intellective competence, a component of instruction that so many educators fail to recognize. KIPP schools provide developmental activities that balance the rigor of college preparatory instruction with field

126

trips and other extracurricular activities, such as sports, music, and arts.

As with other efforts to reform public education, the KIPP program has its skeptics. Observers are critical of the enrollment status, arguing that KIPP students may not truly represent minority and low-income students. This is based on the assumption that the parents of KIPP students are more motivated than average and enrollees are high achievers. Critics say that the commitment of KIPP parents amounts to nothing more than getting the children to school and signing off on their homework. No matter the criticism, KIPP's African American inner-city students are gaining the intellective competence needed to succeed in college preparatory high schools, four-year colleges, and the future. KIPP is closing the achievement gap (KIPP, 2004).

Issues Preventing Implementation

Programs, studies, and analyses have identified various approaches to close the gap. The prototypes are out there and succeeding. All that prevents a more widespread dissemination of the models is the failure of legislative bodies to collaborate with schools, districts, communities, and parents and the commitment of educational leaders to improve and incorporate these methods.

In today's technological society, our national stability rests with the academic achievement of all students, including minority and economically disadvantaged individuals. Academic excellence is our strongest ally as we compete on the global stage.

Our troops must be armed with intelligence, ability, and competency, capable of challenging any threat. To achieve this goal, we must all commit to implementing proven and reachable educational initiatives to eliminate the disparities that responsible for the achievement gap.

CHAPTER 9:
EDUCATING AFRICAN AMERICANS IN THE AGE OF INFORMATION TECHNOLOGY

"Racism is not an excuse to not do the best you can." Arthur Ashe (1943–1993)

Traditionally, methods to improve education stemmed from research gathered and analysis conducted during the age of industrialism. During this time, the focus was on how to prepare young people to succeed in an industrialized age of machinery and equipment. Many African Americans were capable of obtaining gainful employment in various labor-intensive industries. In fact, some industries put aside nationally accepted prejudices and racial discrimination, which allowed African Americans to advance to higher paying labor and supervisory positions. Through on-the-job training and programs that recognized and rewarded seniority, African Americans were able to rise from poverty into blue-collar positions.

With the rapid advances in science and technology, we have transitioned from the industrial age of machinery and equipment to the age of information technology. While machinery and equipment are still fundamental to our economic and social stability, new products are a function, not so much of manpower, but of automation and computers. This era of information technology requires a more intellectual workforce than for which African Americans have traditionally been trained.

The rapid transition into the age of information technology offers the challenge of generating a workforce capable of grasping high level concepts such as physics, mathematics, logic, reasoning, biology, chemistry, and analysis. These subject matters are at the root of automation and information processing. Preparing African American students to meet the challenges of the information technology era is of vital importance.

Kati Haycock, Director, The Education Trust, cites the following two lingering concerns: (The Education Trust, 1999):

- We continue to categorize some students as college bound and others as non-college bound, and then establish different standards and curricula for the two different groups.
- Schools and school districts that serve large concentrations of poor and minority students continue to offer low level curricula, insufficient and out-of-date instructional materials, and teachers that are not educated in the subject matters they are teaching.

These concerns have not been adequately addressed in the context of reducing the achievement gap between minority students and more affluent White students. To achieve the goal of equality and reduce the achievement gap, the age of information technology requires that states make changes in standards and assessments. In the age of industrialism, while White male students were encouraged to excel in "college preparatory'" programs, African American, female, and other minority students were pushed into programs that taught vocational skills and general curriculum knowledge. As a result, White male students were prepared to take white-collar positions while the other students became

corporate America's extensive labor force. After all, blue-collar
positions paid decent salaries, sufficient to support a family. At
the same time, industry was reluctant to accept minorities,
particularly African Americans, in white-collar positions.

This strategy will not work in our current age of information
technology. This era requires *all* students to master skill sets /
necessary to succeed in both the workforce and higher academics.
Education in the age of information technology must implement
proven, documented methods of closing the achievement gap.

While the need will always exist for a service level
workforce, these positions—janitorial, concierge, caretaker, etc.—
do not provide adequate salaries to maintain a decent standard of
living or support a family in today's inflationary economy. For the
African American student who, for years, was considered unworthy
of consideration by the educational system, it is important that
skills development is not geared toward menial, low-paying jobs.
Our educational system is charged with developing skills and
promoting achievement, so it only seems reasonable that we
encourage students to achieve beyond that which sustains poverty.
The skills and knowledge necessary to succeed in college also will
be needed to obtain decent entry level work in the age of
information technology.

Mixed Messages

High school graduation requirements are vastly different
from college entrance requirements. Students, particularly African
American and other minorities, who matriculate through the
existing K–12 system, graduate high school with the false
expectation that they have met the requirements for college.

However, colleges and universities have different, and in most cases, more difficult entrance requirements. Students used to advancing from one grade level to the next find that as college freshmen, they must take remedial coursework just to catch up, extending their college career beyond the traditional two and four years.

This is even more devastating for students who are dependent on financial assistance. Remedial coursework cuts into assistance that is typically provided for four-year programs. These students may find it difficult to complete a traditional college program because the funds run out after the fourth year. Students receiving financial aid may be forced to endure a heavier than normal workload that conflicts with other commitments and priorities to accumulate credits once remedial studies are completed. Educators and educational leaders must redesign standards and assessments so that students can transition from high school to college without the need for remedial training.

K–16 educators must prepare students for the rigors of college and our current age of information technology. Higher education must collaborate with K–16 educators to define what is needed for students to excel. Both entities must train educators to help students reach their goals. Through publishing, the Internet, conferences, etc., educators, administrators, politicians, and the community can share information on proven ways to eliminate the achievement gap.

Rigorous standards will ensure that real goals, not artificial ones, are designed to matriculate students toward a successful college career and beyond. The age of information technology requires that students are capable of critical thinking, analysis, reporting, interpreting, and summarizing. These skills are of such importance that they need to be specifically assessed for every student, at every grade level, K–16.

Assessing the Teacher

Educators, their knowledge and licensing standards, must also be capable of meeting the new and improved standards. Research shows that student achievement is directly linked to teacher quality. Teacher quality must, therefore, include both traditional pedagogical knowledge as well as rigorous content knowledge. Teacher quality is an aspect of education that we have the power to institute and improve.

For African American and other minority students, enhancing teacher quality must also incorporate a systematic approach to collaborative interventions in the school, home, and community. Research has shown that this collaboration is necessary and effective in overcoming the socioeconomic and other cultural differences that exist outside of the school. Collaboration is also necessary to establish a system of effective learning transfers in school and classroom environments. Teacher quality must include, in its definition, the ability to teach for knowledge acquisition, improved comprehension, and deep understanding. These issues were repeatedly ignored during the industrial age and in traditional educational systems, but their inclusion will become a major part of the new programs designed to help students succeed in the age of information technology.

In order to strengthen the educational quality for minority students, the following concerns must be addressed:
When students are taught by teachers and other authority figures that "look like them," performance is enhanced.

In schools highly populated with African American students, the lack of African American teachers and authority figures creates a climate of distrust and suspicion. Students assume that the authority figures will make unfair judgments against them. The threat of being unfairly stereotyped, rejected, and judged creates anxiety in students. Students may openly rebel in this type of environment, particularly when the authority figures make no attempt to tolerate differences in features, behavior and speech.

Students need authority figures that are knowledgeable about their home and community so that they can generate dialogue on pertinent issues. They will not trust or interact with the "strange" authoritarians that seem to be in control of their destinies. As students distance themselves from the strangers, they exclude themselves from academic and social activities. Hire more African American teachers and administrators, and many of these problems will be eliminated.

Teacher licensing and certification tests measure only basic competencies.

Teacher licensing and certification tests are legally required to be psychometrically sound. Past litigations have established that entry-level teaching qualifications must have a direct relevance to the job. For example, a plumber is not required to test for knowledge in trigonometry because he'll never use it to repair pipes. Test questions must be designed to prove compliance with this law of relevance.

Teacher licensing and certification tests are validated to ensure such compliance—and this virtually guarantees a minimal level of skills testing. In 1999, The Education Trust reported that most elementary school teachers were certified based on a tenth grade level of knowledge, and seven states required no assessment for certification (Mitchell, 1999, p. 3). Also, 44 states required examinations for secondary school certification, but only 29 of those states required examinations in subjects that they taught. Furthermore, some states only require a 50 percent passing score, and in districts where school teachers are in short supply, minimum requirements are waived.

Consequently, African American students are most often taught by the least skilled teachers. Not only have their teachers been inadequately educated and assessed, the minimum requirements for their assessments might have been waived.

Some teacher licensing and certification tests are easier than tests taken by high school students.

Attempts to satisfy the legalities of licensing and certification test compliance, rather than student needs, have led to the generalization of teacher assessments. A study by the Education Trust found that most tests are easier than the SAT and ACT (Mitchell, 1999, p. 10). While some certification tests include content beyond the high school level, most never go beyond college sophomore or junior levels.

Traditional philosophies assert that minimal requirements are required for certification.

Traditional methods of teacher training were based on the assumption that teachers only needed basic training and that growth and knowledge, suitable for the subject matter being taught, could

135

be acquired over time (The Education Trust, 1999). Under the influence of industrialism, this outdated philosophy was not without merit. It was reasonable to assume that professional growth could be acquired in time because the standards required of teachers and the curricula were much less rigorous. In our age of information technology, teachers need training in mathematics, technology, and analysis as well as methods of transferring this knowledge to students. This more advanced level of training is required of all new and existing teachers if students are to receive the training they need to function in the age of information technology. Professional development is dependant upon a system that encourages continuous training and collaborations between teachers and other educational professionals.

The new requirements and standards require long-term training.
In the industrial age, as new and advanced machinery was developed, a hands-on training program was sufficient to provide employees with skills to operate machinery and perform other laborious tasks. Teachers satisfactorily taught students to function as laborers. In our age of information technology, fundamental skills in reasoning, analysis, and problem solving are required to operate and control automated systems. The necessary skill sets require a more rigorous learning curve that cannot be easily acquired through traditional education and short-term training programs. These skills are best acquired through an educational system designed to build on intellectual competence. To build intellectual competence teachers must be skilled in developing student achievement over periods of time.

Educating African Americans in the Age of
Information Technology

Panels comprised of novice teachers are, too often, the evaluators of licensing and certification exams.
Evaluation panels are often directed by professionals with less than 5 years of experience (Education Trust, 1999). However, those experiences are based on their work during the age of industrialism. Evaluation panels are outdated and incapable of assessing the skill sets necessary for today's technological applications. Test evaluators must be able to understand how technology is used in the classroom and beyond to accurately evaluate the skills of potential and continuing teachers. They must be able to identify those teachers who are skilled in transferring knowledge in science, mathematics, and reasoning to students. The education system must, then, implement programs to further develop such skills.

Early education researchers did not have the skills or, in the case of low-income and minority students, the concern, to adequately measure variables that affect educational achievement. Improved educational research has clearly identified teacher quality as having a direct impact on student achievement. This research has shown that student test scores increase with increased teacher test scores. In science and math, which are crucial to information technology, student achievement has been shown to increase when teachers have content knowledge in these subject areas.

In the process of developing methods to close the achievement gap that separates African American and other minority students from more affluent students, the country has transitioned from an age of industrialism to the age of information technology. The restructuring of both student and teacher standards to close the achievement gap have been compounded by the need to bring standards in line with the age of information technology.

The proposed standards require the inclusion of rigorous measures, change of focus, the elimination of mixed messaging with regard to standards, and a revision of teacher licensing and certification methods. The changes required are challenging, but they are achievable and attainable.

BIBLIOGRAPHY

Ascher, C. (1992). School Programs for African American Males....and Females, *Phi Delta Kappan*.

Bandura, A. (1993). Perceived self-efficacy in cognitive development and functioning, *Educational Psychology*, 41 (12), 1389–1391.

Bennett, C.I. (1995). *Comprehensive multicultural education, theory, and practice.* Boston: Allyn & Bacon.

Bennett, A., Bridglall, B.L., Cauce, A.M., Everson, H.T., Gordon, E.W., Lee, C.D., et al. (2004). All students reaching the top: Strategies for closing academic achievement gaps (Report of the National Study Group for the Affirmative Development of Academic Ability). Naperville, IL: Learning Point Associates. Retrieved January 7, 2005, from http://www.ncrel.org/gap/studies/thetop.htm.

Boykin, A.W. (1986). *The triple quandary and the schooling of Afro-American children.* In U. Niesser (Ed.), The school achievement of minority children: New Perspectives (pp. 57–92) Hillside, NJ: Lawrence Erlbaum Associates.

Clark, R. (1983). *Family life and school achievement: Why poor black children succeed or fail*, Chicago: University of Chicago Press.

139

Delpit, L. (1995). *Other people's children: Cultural conflict in the classroom*. New York: The New Press.

Department of Education: National center for education statistics. Percentage of students, by reading achievement level and race/ethnicity, grade 4: 1992–2003. Retrieved January 11, 2005 from http://nces.ed.gov/nationsreportcard/reading/results2003/natachieve-re-g4.asp.

Department of Education: National Center for Education Statistics. Percentage of students, by reading achievement level and race/ethnicity, grade 8: 1992–2003 Retrieved January 11, 2005 from http://nces.ed.gov/nationsreportcard/reading/results2003/natachieve-re-g8.asp.

Dietal, D. (2004). "Helping your Child Perform Well on Tests." *Our Children*, 27, 7–8.

The Education Trust. (1999). *Thinking K–16: Ticket to Nowhere, The Gap Between Leaving High School and Entering College and High Performance Jobs*, Retrieved January 8, 2005 from www2.edtrust.org.

The Education Trust. (1999). *Not Good Enough: A Content Analysis of Teacher Licensing Examinations*. Retrieved June 8, 2005 from www2.edtrust.org.

The Education Trust. (2002). Education Watch: The Nation: Key education facts and figures: Achievement, attainment, and opportunity: Retrieved January 11, 2005. Page 10–11. Retrieved January 11, 2005 from www2.edtrust.org/edtrust.org.

Bibliography

Ferguson, Ronald F. (1998a). "Teachers' Perceptions and Expectations and the Black-White Test Score Gap." Pp. 273–145 in Christopher Jencks and Meredith Phillips (Eds.), The Black-White Test Score Gap. Washington, DC: Brookings Institutions Press.

Gay, G. (2000). *Culturally responsive teaching: Theory, research, and practice*. New York: Teachers College Press.

Gazin, Ann. (2004, August). What do you expect? A teacher's high—or low—expectations can wield a profound influence on students. Here's how to set the bar high for every child. *Instructor,* v114, i1, p18(4).

Goodenow, C. & Grady, K.E. (1994). The relationship of school belonging and friends' values to academic motivation among urban adolescent students, *Journal of Experimental Education,* 62 (1), 60–71.

Graybill, Susan W. (1997). Questions of race and culture: how they relate to the classroom for African American students. *The Clearing House,* v70, n6, p311(8).

Hale, Janice E. (1982). *Black Children: Their Roots, Culture, and Learning Styles*, Brigham Young University Press.

Hale-Benson, Janice E. (1986). *Black Children: Their Roots, Culture, and Learning Styles*, Baltimore, MD: Johns Hopkins University Press.

141

Horgan, D.D. (1995). *Achieving gender equity: Strategies for the classroom.* Boston: Allyn & Bacon.

Kiviat, B.J. (2001). Pioneers of Advocacy: The Social Side of Schooling. Johns Hopkins Magazine. Retrieved January 11, 2005, from http://www.jhu.edu/~jhumag/0400web/18.html.

Kiviat, B.J. (2001). Pioneers of Advocacy: The Social Side of Schooling. Johns.

Hopkins Magazine. Retrieved January 11, 2005, from http://www.jhu.edu/~jhumag/0400web/18.html.

King, J.E. (1994). *The purpose of schooling for African American children: Including cultural knowledge in teaching diverse populations.* Albany: State University of New York Press.

KIPP. (2004). *Knowledge Is Power Program: Schools in Action.* Retrieved May 20, 2005 from http://www.kipp.org/schoolsinaction.cfm?pageid=nav1.

Knapp, M., Turnbull, B., Shields, P. (1995, June). Academic challenge in high-poverty classrooms. *Phi Delta Kappan,* v76, n10, p770(7).

Kochman, T. (1981). *Black and White styles in conflict.* Chicago: University of Chicago Press.

Kunjufu, Jawanza. (1989). *A Talk with Jawanza: Critical Issues in Educating African American Youth,* Chicago: African American Images.

Bibliography

Kunjufu, Jawanza. (2002). *Black Students. Middle Class Teachers.* Chicago: African American Images.

Kunjufu, Jawanza. (2004). *Countering the Conspiracy to Destroy Black Boys.* Chicago: African American Images.

Kunjufu, Jawanza. (1984). *Developing positive self-images and discipline in black children.* Chicago: African American Images.

Kunjufu, Jawanza. (1986). *Motivating and Preparing Black Youth for Success.* Chicago: African American Images.

Ladson-Billings, G. (1995a). But that's just good teaching! The case for culturally relevant pedagogy. *Theory Into Practice,* 34, 159–164.

Ladson-Billings, G. (1995b). Toward a theory of culturally relevant pedagogy. *American Educational Research Journal,* 32, 465–491.

Mitchell, R. and Barthe, P. (1999) Thinking K–16: Not Good Enough, *How Teacher Licensing Tests Fall Short.* The Education Trust, Vol. 3 Issue 1 p3.

Murphy's Laws Site. (2002). *Murphy's Laws.* Retrieved May 22, 2005 from http://www.murphys-laws.com/murphy/murphy-laws.html.

NCREL. (2003). Perspectives on Gap: Fostering the Academic Success of Minority and Low-Income Students. Retrieved January 11, 2005 from www.ncrel.org.

Obiakor, Festus E. (1999). "Teacher Expectations of Minority Exceptional Learners: Impact on Accuracy of Self-Concepts." *Exceptional Children,* v66 i1 p39.

Obiakor, Festus E., & Ford, Bridgie A., editors. (2002). *Creating Successful Learning Environments for African American Learners with Exceptionalities*, California: Corwin Press, Inc.

Ogbu, J. (1978). "Why Blacks Do Poorly in School." *American and World Wide News*, July 10.

Ogbu, J. (2003). *Black American Students in an Affluent Suburb*: A Study of Academic Disengagement. Mahwah, New Jersey: Lawrence Erlbaum Associates.

Phillips, M., Crouse, J., & Ralph, J. (1998). Does the Black-White test score gap widen after children enter school? In C. Jencks & M. Phillips (Eds.), The Black-White test score gap (pp. 229–272). Washington, DC: Brookings Institute Press.

Powell, G.J. (1983). America's minority group children: The underserved. Prologue in The psychosocial development of minority group children. New York: Brunner/Mazel.

Rosenthal, R., & Jacobson, L. (1968). *Pygmalion Effect in the Classroom: Teacher Expectation and pupils' intellectual development.* New York: Holt, Rhinehart and Watson.

Sadker, M., & D. Sadker. (1994). *Failing at fairness: How America's schools cheat girls.* New York: Charles Scribner's Sons.

Bibliography

Schunk, D.H. (1996). Learning theories (2nd ed.). Englewood Cliffs, NJ: Prentice Hall.

Seal, D., Stipek, K. (2001). *Motivated Minds.* New York: New York Henry Holt and Company.

Taylor, R., & Reeves, J. (1993). More is better: Raising expectations for students at risk. *Middle School Journal,* 24, 13–18.

Tucker, Carolyn M. (1999). *African American Children: A self-empowerment approach to modifying behavioral problems and preventing academic failure.* Massachusetts: Allyn & Bacon.

U. S. Department of Education. (2005). *Helping your Child with Homework.* Jessup, Maryland: Ed Pubs.

Villegas, A.M. (1991). Culturally responsive pedagogy for the 1990s and beyond (Trends and Issues Paper No. 6). Washington, DC: ERIC Clearinghouse on Teacher Education.

Wong, H.K. (1998). The *First Days of School.* Mountainview, California: Harry K. Wong Publications, Inc.

Woodson, Carter G. (1933). *The Miseducation of the Negro,* Washington, DC: Associated Press.

SUGGESTED READING

Alexander, K.L., & Entwise, D.R. (1988). Achievement in the first 2 years of school: Patterns and processes. *Monographs of the Society for Research in Child Development*, 53, 2.

Baratz, S.S. & J.C. (1969). Negro Ghetto Children and Urban Education: A cultural solution, *Social Education*, 33:400–404.

Baruth, L.G., and M.L. Manning. (1992). *Multicultural education of children and adolescents*. Needham Heights, MA.: Allyn and Bacon.

Boykin, A.W. (1982). Task variability and the performance of black and white school children, In J. Spence (Ed.), *Achievement and achievement motives*, San Francisco: Freeman.

Boykin, A.W. (1983). The academic performance of Afro-American children, In J. Spence (Ed.), *Achievement and achievement motives,* San Francisco: Freeman.

Brophy, J., & Good, T. (1974). *Teacher-student relationships: Causes and consequences*. New York: Holt, Rinehart, & Winston.

Bronfenbrenner, U. (1979). *The ecology of human development*. Cambridge: Harvard University Press.

Suggested Reading

Chimezie, A. (1988). Black children's characteristics and the school: A selective adaptation approach, *The Western Journal of Black Studies*, 12, 77–85.

Cole, M. & others. (1971). *The Cultural Context of Thinking and Learning*, New York: Basic Books.

Cooper, H.M. (1979). Pygmalion grows up: A model for teacher expectation communication and performance influence, *Review of Educational Research*, 49, 389–410.

Cooper, H.M., & Tom, D.Y.H. (1984). Teacher expectation research: A review with implications for classroom instruction. *Elementary School Journal*, 85, 77–89.

Delpit, L.D. (1988). The silenced dialogue: Power and pedagogy in educating other people's children. *Harvard Educational Review*, 58(3), 280–297.

Dillon, D.R. (1989). Showing them that I want them to learn and that I care about who they are: A micro ethnography of the social organization of a secondary low-track English-reading classroom. *American Educational Research Journal*, 26(2), 227–259.

Ford, D.Y. (1998, Spring). The under representation of minority students in gifted education: Problems and promises in recruitment and retention. *The Journal of Special Education*, 32, 4–14.

Fordham, S., and Ogbu, J. (1986). Black Students School Success: Coping With Burden of Acting White. The Urban Review, Vol. 18, No. 3.

Foster, M. (1992). Sociolinguistics and the African-American community: Implications for literacy. *Theory Into Practice*, 31(4): 303–310.

Franklin, Mary E. (1992). Culturally sensitive instructional practices for African-American learners with disabilities. *Exceptional Children*, v59, n2, p115 (8).

Gay, G. (1978). Multicultural preparation and teacher effectiveness in desegregated schools. *Theory Into Practice*, 11, 149–156.

Gay, G. (1995). A multicultural school curriculum. In C. A. Grant & M. Gomez (Eds.), Making school multicultural: Campus and classroom (pp. 37–54). Englewood Cliffs, NJ: Merrill/ Prentice Hall.

Gay, G. (2000). *Culturally responsive teaching: Theory, research, and practice.* New York: Teachers College Press.

Gibbs, J.T. (1988). *Young, black, and male in America: An endangered species.* Dover, MA.: Auburn.

Gilbert, S.E., and Gay, G. (1985). Improving the success in school of poor black children. *Phi Delta Kappan,* 67(2): 133–37.

Good, T.L., & Brophy, J.E. (1986). School effects. In M.C. Wittrock (ed., *Handbook of research on teaching*, (3rd ed.), New York: Macmillan.

Gotts, E., & Purnell, R. (1987). Practicing school-family relations in urban settings, *Education and Urban Society*, 19(2), 212–218.

Graham, S. (1994, Spring). Motivation in African Americans. *Review of Educational Research*, 64, 55–117.

Graham, S. (1997). Using attribution theory to understand social and academic motivation in African American youth. *Educational Psychologist*, 32, 21–34.

Guttentag, M. (1972). Negro-White Differences in Children's Movement. *Perpetual and Motor Skills*, 35:435–36.

Hall, V.C., Howe, A., Merkel, A., & Lederman, N. (1986). Behavior, motivation, and achievement in desegregated junior high school classes, *Journal of Educational Psychology*, 78(2), 108–115.

Hollins, E.R., King, J.E., & Hayman, W.C. (Eds.). (1994). *Teaching* ✓ *diverse populations: Formulating a knowledge base*. Albany: State University of New York Press.

Horgan, D.D. (1995). *Achieving gender equity: Strategies for the classroom*. Boston: Allyn & Bacon.

✓ Howard, G.R. (1999). *We can't teach what we don't know: White teachers, multiracial schools*. New York: Teachers College Press.

Irvine, J.J. (1990). Black students and school failure. Westport, CT: Greenwood.

Kochman, T. (1981). *Black and White styles in conflict.* Chicago: University of Chicago Press.

Kuykendall, Crystal. (1989). Improving Black Student Achievement By Enhancing Students' Self-Image. Mid-Atlantic Equity Center, Chevy Chase, MD.

Lee, C. (in press). The Educability of Intellective Competence. In E.W. Gordon & B. L. Bridglall (Eds.), *The affirmative development of academic ability.* Lanham, MD: Rowman and Littlefield.

Locke, D.C. (1992). *African Americans. In Increasing multicultural understanding: A comprehensive model.* Multicultural Aspects of Counseling Series. Newbury Park, Calif.: Sage.

Lomotey, K. (ed. 1990). *Prologue in Going to school: The African-American experience.* Albany, N.Y.: State University of New York Press.

Norton, D.G. (1983). *Black family life patterns, the development of self and cognitive development of black children.* In The psychosocial development of minority group children, edited by G. J. Powell, 181–93. New York: Brunner/Mazel.

Suggested Reading

Obiakor, F.E. (1992). Self-concept of African American students: An operational model for special education. Exceptional Children, 59, 160–167.

Obiakor, F.E. (1994). The eight-step multicultural approach: Learning and teaching with a smile. Dubuque, IA: Kendall/Hunt.

Paley, Vivian G. (1979). *White Teacher*, Harvard University Press, Cambridge, MA.

Parillo, V.N. (1980). *Strangers to these shores: Race and ethnic relations in the United States*. Boston: Houghton Mifflin.

Poplin, M.S. (1988). Holistic/constructivist principles of the teaching/learning process: Implications for the field of learning disabilities. *Journal of Learning Disabilities*, 21(7), 401–416.

Powell-Hobson, D., & Hobson, D.S. (1992). *Different and wonderful: Raising Black children in a race-conscious society*. Boston: Houghton Mifflin.

Rankin, P. (1967). *The relationship between parent behavior and achievement of inner-city elementary school children*, Paper presented at American Educational Research Association Convention, New York.

Skinner, E.A., Zimmer-Gembeck, M.J., & Connell, J.P. (1998). *Individual differences and the development of perceived control*. In Monographs of the Society for Research in Child Development (Vol. 63, Serial No. 254). Chicago: The University of Chicago Press.

Slavin, R.E., & Madden, N.A. (1979). School practices that improve race relations. *American Educational Research Journal*, 16, 169–180.

Slavin R.E., & Oickle, E. (1981). Effects of cooperative learning teams on student achievement and race relations: Treatment by race interactions. *Sociology of Education*, 54, 174–180.

Spindler, G.D. (Ed.). (1987). Education and cultural process: Anthropological approaches (2nd ed.). Prospect Heights, IL: Waveland.

Tatum, Alfred W. (2000). Breaking down barriers that disenfranchise African American adolescent readers in low-level tracks. *Journal of Adolescent & Adult Literacy*, v44, i1 p52.

Tharp, R.G. (1989). Psychocultural variables and constants: Effects on teaching and learning in schools. *American Psychologist*, 44(2), 349–359.

Tucker, C.M., Y.R. Harris, Brady, B.A., & Herman, K.C. (1997). The association of selected parent behaviors with the academic achievement of African American children and European American children, *Child Study Journal*, 26(4), 253–277.

Tucker, C.M., Herman, K., Brady, B.A., & Fraser, K., (1995). Operation positive expression: A behavior change program for adolescent halfway house residents, *Residential Treatment for Children and Youth*, 13(2), 67–80.

Suggested Reading

Williams, D., & Chavkin, N. (1985). *Final report of the parent involvement education project,* Contract No. 400-83-007, Project P-2, Washington, DC: National Institute of Education.

Wright, W.J. (1991). The endangered black male child. *Educational Leadership.* 49(4): 14–16.

NOTES

NOTES

NOTES

NOTES

NOTES

NOTES

NOTES

NOTES

NOTES

NOTES

NOTES

NOTES

NOTES